CATBIN FEVER

CATBIN FEVER is based on, and from the creator of, the hit Twitter account @CatBinLady as seen on Channel 4 News.

Praise for @CatBinLady :-

"...the pleasure she has afforded us all is a marvellous thing..." - India Knight, The Sunday Times

"...a huge online hit." - Andy Crick, The Sun

"Whatever you do, follow @CatBinLady" - Claudia Winkleman

"You all already know this, but @CatBinLady is one of the funniest/best conceived things I've seen on Twitter." - Chris Addison

"Everything about her is great." - Graham Linehan

"Well funny." - Jason Manford

"We love you CatBinLady" - Adult Swim UK

CatBinLady was among NME's 25 best Twitter moments of 2010

CatBinLady won the 2011 Loaded LAFTA for Funniest Twitterer.

CATBIN FEVER

By Rich Neville

ISBN 978-0-9570827-1-7
Published by Furious Snowball

catbinfever.com

CONTENTS

GNOME..9

OUTING..14

DESCENDING..19

KANYE..23

BIRTHDAY..25

RESPONSIBILITY...28

MOURNING..34

REUNITING..42

WATCHING..49

COURTING...55

JOBSEEKING...60

SERVICING..66

SIBLING...70

STALKING..78

CELEBRATING...82

LISTING..87

FESTIVE..97

THEATRE..104

SLIMMING..106

RECREATION..110

EASTER...115

WEDDING...119

SCOURGING...123

"I have momentary aberrations. We all do."

1

GNOME

NO ENTRY is written across the sliding doors I've just gone through, so that's not right for a start. They made a noise when I was pulling at them and now they won't shut again. Running up the drinks aisle, I am able to find a member of staff, but only just before a small child tries to enter the supermarket the wrong way. I have barely enough time to point out the child and shout 'that's awful', before its mother pulls it back out onto the pavement. The staff member is young, and is wearing a badge with 'Michael' written on it. So that's either his name, or the name of a band he likes. I don't know why he thinks I would be interested in the information either way. Possibly-Michael goes off to wrestle with the doors before any more children try to get in, so I've done everything I can here. No good deed goes unpunished though, and I have to walk right the way to the other end of the supermarket to find a trolley.

I wander the aisles largely without incident, acquiring my provisions. As I reach the cereals, I place some frozen sausages between the porridge and the own-brand corn flakes. They'll probably go off there before they are discovered. I draw no pleasure from this.

While I queue at the checkout, I have the strangest feeling that I've forgotten something. It's very unnerving.

Groceries bought, I hit the high street. I thank possibly-Michael for holding the doors as I pass him. I've had to pay a pound for this trolley, but it's worth it, as I've done my big shop for the week. The trolley lets me make my way up the high street at a fair rate. Some bits of Coventry are very nice to wander slowly through, but this isn't one of them, because of Hitler. Passing a shoe shop, I stop to investigate some of the sample shoes sat on a rack just outside the door. One in particular catches my eye, a purple suede wedge, and I throw it on top of a bus. Why do I do these things? No-one has noticed me, except for an old woman and a small child on the bus itself. They stare accusingly through the windows and in return I show them the finger. There are a lot of people getting on, so this stand-off seems to last an eternity before the bus finally pulls away.

As I head for home, I'm struck by an unavoidable truth. It means I'll have to carry the bags most of the way back, but this trolley is going in the canal. I wait for some skateboarding youths and a cyclist to pass before I emerge from the bushes and push it off the towpath. If they'd witnessed this, they wouldn't understand. How could they? I'm not sure I do, and I've just done it. Peering in, I can't even see the trolley. It's a disgrace. They should clean up this water. And I won't get that pound back now. Last year, the supermarket tried offering customers a two pound reward for information leading to the recovery of their trolleys, but people just took advantage and spent all day borrowing them for a pound and hiding them. I heard one man made over three hundred pounds off the one trolley before they cottoned on. It's awful if that's true. It's because of people like him that this will go unreported.

As I turn the corner into my road with my very heavy bags, I see that number 35 hasn't taken her milk in again. I really feel like pouring it through her letterbox for her. What am I like? I take a few deep breaths and walk on. Her slovenliness is none of my concern.

Next door's gnome glares at me as I struggle up the path with the shopping. Other than that, it feels good to be home. I put everything away and relax with a nice cup of tea. Half an hour later, I have kicked the head off next door's gnome. For a joke. But who's laughing now? Not me. Not me.

***

I put on my glad rags and apply some fresh lipstick, because I'm meeting Brenda for an evening at the social club, now that it has reopened. I have always found the majority of the people there to be very judgemental and right up themselves, but not Brenda. I think she may be the best friend I've ever had.

As I enter the club, I can already feel the stares. I compliment Bill the barman on the refurbishment, and he thanks me in turn for making it necessary. At least someone in here appreciates what I did. Brenda waves from the corner. She has had her hair done, and draws attention to the fact by making a play of patting at it with her palms. I'm thinking what a scandal it is that hairdressing is still unregulated in this country, but I don't say anything. The important thing is that she likes it. She moves some of her scratch cards to allow room for my drink. We talk about our respective days as she scratches. Brenda suggests that I should pop a note or a card in next door about the gnome. I point out that this might seem like gloating, but then she explains that she means the note should be by way of an apology. She's given me a lot to think about. I hope she wins ten pounds one day.

***

Home again. As I come in the door, I realise I've still got the black ball from the social club pool table in my coat pocket. I don't even know why I wanted it. There's a note waiting for me on the mat. It's from next door, wondering whether I saw any youths in the area this evening. I don't have time to be counting youths for them, whatever survey they're doing. I decide against the note Brenda was suggesting, as I don't want to end up getting involved in their statistic gathering. They aren't even members of our neighbourhood watch.

I take the rubbish out, but before I know what I'm doing, I've swung the bag round and flung it over the fence. I think it's in their tree. WHY?

2

OUTING

Today is the day of the church social outing. We're visiting the medieval market town of Shrewsbury. God alone knows why. Brenda can't make it, but I visit her for a morning coffee. She hands me a card with a sad-looking kitten on, and the word 'sorry' in gold script. She suggests this might be suitable for the gnome situation. She says she's bought me a whole box of them. I'm not at all sure about this, but I take the cards so as not to hurt her feelings. While the kettle is boiling, Brenda shows me a picture on her fridge that her goddaughter has done. I don't say anything, but I do hope she's been punished for it. At least I know now that Brenda isn't doing those pictures herself. Originally I had thought it to be some kind of cry for help. Poor

Brenda is very put-upon by her goddaughter's mother. When a person agrees to be a godparent, I'm sure the last thing they expect is to be burdened with a child on a regular basis by its bewildered owner when they should be going to Shrewsbury. Brenda is a saint to put up with it all, she really is.

We have a lovely cup of coffee, but as soon as Brenda pops to the little girls' room to powder her nose, I tip the remainder of mine down the back of her telly. I'm already regretting this as she returns. I hand her one of the sad kitten cards as I leave for the coach station.

***

All the usual suspects are waiting as I arrive at the station. I buy myself a puzzle magazine and a juice carton for the journey and make my way to the back of the coach, as I enjoy making gestures to other road users. Having both hands free is a joy when you're not driving. Almost everyone gestures back. The dual carriageway is like a mobile community. I don't understand why none of the other ladies ever join in. At one point, Tony the driver asks me to turn round and sit properly, for safety. I stare at him in his rear view mirror as I have my juice, and he eventually decides that what I was doing was safe after all.

Maureen and Bernadette are giggling to each other behind me as we walk from the car park in Shrewsbury. They are very full of themselves because they were on that show on telly once, where people invite each other round for dinner and an argument. Bernadette only did a roast, and I have it on good authority that Maureen got all her pasta dishes from a local restaurant. Bernadette didn't have it in her own flat, either. She's in sheltered accommodation. They follow me into the first tea shop I come across, but we don't share a table. I watch as they order a full cream tea with scones, despite Bernadette having claimed not to be able to digest cream on the programme. She is a liar. This is a stunning revelation. I would have expected this of Maureen, but not Bernadette. I only had her down as lazy before. And perhaps a little loose. I also have scones, but I never said I couldn't, so there's nothing wrong in that. The whole time we're sat in the tea shop, I look daggers at Bernadette and mouth the word 'liar'. Once or twice I scoop a bit of cream onto my middle finger and show it to her, so she knows what I'm talking about. She knows. She must know. It's written all over her face. It clearly affects her enjoyment of the scones, and they leave before I do, with their tails between their legs. As I'm waiting at the till to pay, I remember that it was a different woman from Stoke who couldn't have cream.

***

I'm back on the coach before anyone else. If they don't want

16

people to do what I've just done in the gallery, then they shouldn't sell marker pens in the gift shop. Feeling indignant.

Feeling a bit lonely.

I've done quite a few puzzles from my book by the time the coach fills up again. I've used the windows and the back of the seat in front for workings. I am surrounded by numbers, and feel like a brainy mathematician. This perks me up a bit as the coach moves off.

An hour later, and we are waiting for a relief coach at the services because some of the tyres were flat when everyone came back from their toilet break. I can feel several of the church social ladies staring at me. Maureen and Bernadette are whispering. It's plain rudeness.

When I eventually get home, her from across the way comes over shouting the odds, looking for her wind chimes. I tell her I don't have them. I don't. They're on her roof, where I threw them. I think she's some kind of new age hippy, but she certainly doesn't seem very peaceful. She is some piece of work, coming over here, making nasty insinuations. I wouldn't put it past her to be doing black magic over there, I really wouldn't.

Number 35 has even more milk outside her door now. There's no excuse for it. This is a nice neighbourhood, and some people are just dragging it down.

I'm a bit surprised Brenda hasn't rung this evening, what with her telly being bust. You would think she'd want the company.

3

DESCENDING

At my niece's birthday party. The cake's in the pond. It's not going down as well as I thought.

Once I had the idea at the hostess trolley, the whole project came together very quickly, as the patio doors were already open and a lot of the guests were outside. From my perspective, the only thing that could have improved it would have been the sponge expanding and soaking up all the water. But this isn't a perfect world. Nothing from this crowd, though. Pearls before swine. Before I know it, I'm being ushered back into the house by Susan. She's saying she's not angry, but that she thinks perhaps I should leave. I know that this is really about me forgetting to bring her a present. She is an avaricious piece of work.

I tell Brenda about my morning over coffee. I tell her she would have laughed if she had been there, and she eventually accepts this as a possibility. That's why we get along so well. We both have a sense of humour.

Brenda pops to the toilet and the replacement telly is just staring at me. This is killing me. Part of me knows we'd both fall about if she came back down to find me stood over the telly with an empty coffee mug, but I think she wants to watch David Attenborough later. I weather the temptation and leave it, despite the heavy knowledge that it will never be as funny having not done it at the first available opportunity. I hope she enjoys her wildlife programme, I really do.

On the way home, I realise I've accidentally walked off with the remote control for Brenda's new telly, and while I'm bringing it back, my car runs over it. I pop the bits through her door, wrapped in a sad kitten card.

***

It's the following morning, and I'm having brunch in town. There's a rude word on the window of this café written in squirty ketchup. I think the owner thinks I did it. I know I did. Embarrassed. She's stood there behind the counter, arms folded. Judging me. The dripping word I'm sat under is something I'd never say. People are looking in. This is the tensest egg batch I've ever eaten.

My nerves are rattled. Before making the journey home, I decide to try to relax at the cinema. I like to stand quite close to the screen, but people are complaining. Why can't they let me be?

***

Back home, and I have taken in next door's washing for them because it looks like rain, but now it has writing on it. On reflection, I decide it might be best to simply stuff it into their hedge. When and if they find it, they will probably think the wind took it, and will hopefully assume they'd simply never noticed the swearing on his work shirts. The young people in those sweatshops probably swear on the clothing all the time, like they do on the walls in town. It's a disgrace, if that's true.

***

Sunday rolls around, and at church this morning I enjoyed the sermon, but kept showing the vicar the finger every time I caught his eye. Not sure he 'got' it. Mortified if not. I like to think a man of the cloth would be blessed with a strong sense of humour, though. It stands to reason. He's normally at the door to meet everyone on the way out, but not today.

I've invited Brenda round for a Sunday roast. It has gone very well. I wrapped the chicken in bacon and it came out lovely, I told her, and she agreed. She couldn't tell me what trimmings were, but apparently we had them all. She didn't finish her dessert so I've poured it into her handbag. She can have it later.

4

KANYE

The Grammy Award-winning rapper Kanye West is a great source of comfort to me. Kanye doesn't let anyone tell him what to do. Not even in writing. He once described himself as 'a proud non-reader of books'. This gives him what he calls 'a childlike purity'. I like to think I have that as well, although I must confess to having read several novels. I like crime thrillers best. I would never write one though. Not after Kanye said that people who write novels 'just be so wordy and so self-absorbed'. I would be crushed if he thought that of me. Like Kanye, I cannot abide people who are right up themselves. It must be said, though, that he is a bit more outspoken than I could be. I don't like to upset people. He isn't afraid to stand up and be counted when he sees injustice, which I find very inspiring. When Kanye saw that the award for the best music video featuring a woman was about to be mistakenly given to the wrong person, because there was another woman who had appeared in a better video, he stepped up without a second thought. There's an important lesson there. Sometimes you just have to act on instinct, without regard for the consequences. You have to ask yourself, 'If not me, then who?'

I was introduced to Kanye through an exciting article in a local newspaper that Brenda told me about, which explained that he had decided to follow just one person on something called Twitter, and that they were from Coventry. I had to join up, just to find out if it was me he had his eye on. It wasn't me though, and I must have pressed something, because now I follow him, and I don't know how to stop.

I've not heard any of his rapping, but I'm sure it's very good.

5

BIRTHDAY

We are bowling to celebrate Brenda's birthday. It's half-price on a Wednesday afternoon. Brenda is complaining about the shoes I got her while she was buying the drinks. I had to approximate her feet at the counter and not wanting to get anything too tight, went with size 14s. They are quite large and clown-like on her, and they make a clapping sound when she takes her run-up. People are looking. It's a bit embarrassing.

We've got the rails up on the aisle, which makes it a bit more interesting, as you can bounce the ball off the sides several times before it goes into the pins, if you throw it hard enough. It's important not to miss the rail though. I scored a strike several lanes away earlier, and it didn't come up on our screen at all, so I didn't get those points.

I've just got a half-strike, but I can't complete it as Brenda's bag seems to have jammed in the ball return mechanism. Brenda is flapping off down the lane after it. A man in a suit is following her. I think he may be the manager.

All I can do is sip my drink and watch as Brenda argues with the man and tugs at her handbag. Momentarily the bag is freed, and we are informed that our lane has been closed for repairs.

For a joke, I have told Brenda that the bowling alley has lost her shoes. She has believed me and stormed out of the building like an enraged penguin. I'm now regretting it a bit though, as she is trying to drive us home in the very large clown shoes. I don't feel entirely safe. She can't really operate the pedals one at a time.

***

Back at Brenda's in one piece, and she's just shown me a birthday card she's received from her goddaughter. She's gone to look for some sellotape now.

Feeling a little guilty. In some ways, I don't think the day has been made special enough for Brenda. It was my birthday recently, and Brenda gave me a lady shaver, which I tested on her living room carpet. While she's gone, I book us a table at the golf club for a slap-up dinner. When she comes back down I tell her, and the way her face lights up is reward enough for my efforts. Especially when I offer to pay for my own food.

**

I always enjoy our visits to the golf club. Neither of us play, but there is a lovely ambience at the clubhouse, and they do some wonderful food. After we have been seated for a while, I catch the waiter's eye and ask him about a couple of unusual things on the menu. He doesn't seem to like them, and asks me if I also drew the large one in the toilets. Discretion being the better part of valour, I deny this. It's Brenda's day, after all, and sometimes the work is more important than taking the credit for it.

After our meal, we enjoy a post-dinner coffee in front of a lovely open fire. Very cosy. Brenda is asking the waiter for some tongs so she can retrieve her bag.

6

RESPONSIBILITY

N ext door have asked me to water their plants while they're away, but I only have a vague idea how far I threw their keys after I waved them off. Why me?

I waste several valuable minutes looking for their keys before I give up and decide to think laterally. After a cup of tea and a sit-down, I'm in their porch. I can see a couple of the plants from the letterbox, but the hose isn't reaching very well. I don't need this. Stepping back into the garden, I am aware of a poorly glued gnome staring at me and judging my efforts to be a good neighbour. With a flash of inspiration, I put the gnome through the front window and climb in. From the inside, it's a simple matter to pull the hose through the letterbox and give the plants all the water they could possibly need, and more.

After I turn the outside tap off, I survey my work back indoors with a degree of pride. It can't be denied, however, that there has been collateral damage. Some of the paint has run on a watercolour portrait of the family, obscuring their heads. The clearly shoddy artwork is hanging in the hallway, opposite a small under-stair office area. I note the good use of space, and the presence of a shredder, which is not a toy. I hold my hand to my face so as not to be tempted by the shredder, and find a black felt tip pen on the computer desk in the cubby-hole that I deem suitable to put faces back on my neighbours. It's harder than it seems, as I quickly realise I can't remember whether he has a moustache, or whether she has hair, or indeed whether the children have glasses. When someone lives next door, you don't need to make note of these things, as they're easily identifiable by their location. I know I'm never going to get everything exactly right, so I resolve to make them all bald with glasses and moustaches. At least that way I know some of the details are bound to match. I've not drawn very much since school, and quite enjoy this experience. They are all smiling approvingly once I am finished, and that in a way is thanks enough. Being careful once more not to look at the shredder, which is not a toy, I replace the pen and turn to leave. As I do so, I can see most of the gnome's face lying in the living room, looking out into the hallway at me. He's seen everything. He knows I'm a good neighbour now. I smile and go, being careful to close the front door behind me.

In the evening, I meet Brenda for a quiet drink at the social club. She has come out with her pudding handbag, and it smells quite bad now. Sometimes I surprise myself with my own loyalty. It takes a good friend to sit and say nothing in the face of such a stench. I hope against hope no one thinks it's me.

***

Come morning, I go in to sort next door's mail, but in no time at all I've shredded things I ought not have. I try to draw them some new certificates. I guess the grades. And the subjects. If anything I'm probably too generous with my estimates, but I always try to see the good in people. I heard they were getting straight A's, but I'd be surprised if they can do any of the other letters. I assume the boy one will have done Woodwork, Metalwork and PE, as he is a boy. He will have done satisfactorily in PE as long as he ran in the right direction. He hasn't cut anything off himself to the best of my knowledge, so he may have passed the others. The girl one will probably have done Needlework, Cooking and Poetry. She doesn't seem to close her mouth at any point while talking, so I imagine oral tests won't have gone well, but she may have passed a written exam, as long as she didn't drool too much on the paper.

I slide the new certificates into the envelopes the originals came in and tape them closed, imagining the tension as the family gather round the breakfast table to open them. What's in the envelopes now will doubtless exceed the parents' limited expectations for their ungifted offspring. They will probably celebrate at a burger shop. I picture the slack-jawed children handing their new qualifications over the counter and perhaps even getting jobs there and then. I've made lives better this morning.

As I'm climbing out through the living room window, I pause to admire the mounted butterfly display case on the wall. It occurs to me that there are several dead wasps on my bathroom window sill that may interest them, and I resolve to pop them in an envelope and put them through their letterbox later.

***

A couple of days later, I pop into town with Brenda. While we're in Oxfam searching for some new ensembles with which to wow them at the social club, Brenda feels the call of nature and hands me her coat to look after while she visits the ladies. It's a bit heavy, so I pop it on one of the hangers. By the time she emerges another customer is attempting to purchase her coat and she ends up in a bidding war. It's a bit of a scene, so I go and wait outside.

While we're in Smiths, which is a jumped-up newsagents, I think back on the Oxfam incident and decide Brenda should have a little treat to make up, so I pop the first small thing I spot in her pocket, for her to discover later, knowing the smile the surprise will give her. I think it's a printer cartridge of some sort. I'm not sure if she has a printer gun for it to go in, but she can always buy one of those herself.

On the way out, the store alarm goes off. Several men want to talk to Brenda for some reason, and I have to visit my niece again, so I ask them to tell Brenda I'll see her later.

When I arrive at my niece's house, I present her with her belated birthday gift of some books I got out at the library on the way over. She is complaining that they aren't all in English. She's impossible to please, because Margaret and David have spoiled her absolutely rotten. I don't know why I bother. I return home dejected.

Next door are back. Her next door is saying that the fox I've been throwing dog food into their lounge for isn't even theirs. I'm feeling very deceived. I agree with her that what the vandals have done to their house is just awful. It really is, the way she tells it. I tell her that I'm just glad I wasn't there watering the plants when it happened, and she eventually agrees that this is something to be thankful for.

In the evening I head over to Brenda's. Without the remote, her telly is now stuck on something called 'Kerrang radio' and it's very loud. Still, it's company for her. I remember to give her back her library card, which I think cheers her up a little.

.

7

MOURNING

It's very dark. There's a strange, spooky noise coming from
next door's garden. I'm not scared. I'm making it.

I'm possibly over-excited, as I have been invited to a funeral
tomorrow. It turns out number 35 wasn't just being lazy not
taking in her milk all these weeks after all. Her son and his wife
came over this afternoon and explained that she had passed away
in front of the telly, and as a good friend and neighbour I might
want to attend the service tomorrow. I am a good neighbour, and I
explained as much. Apparently her name was Janet something.
There's going to be an open casket. I might try to pop something
in there, like a time capsule, so when people dig her up in the
future they'll be able to see what things were like. I'd like to

make it seem as if we were more advanced than we are, but I'm not entirely sure how to achieve that. They used to have these time capsules on Blue Peter, which was a BBC programme for teaching middle class children about death, and making things from toilet rolls. They also used to have a very funny section set in their garden. Perhaps I could do something with toilet rolls. My mind is racing. Next door's kitchen light eventually goes off again, and I return to my house still too wired to sleep.

***

In the morning, myself and several of the other neighbours gather at the Sacred Heart church. It seems number 35 was a Catholic. They are a bit like the Church of England, but their priests are all men and aren't allowed to sleep with adults. They also have better communion biscuits that turn into actual bits of flesh. I hope I'll get to see that today. I thought I was going to be late because of a big tailback on the way to the church, but it turned out they were all coming here too, just very slowly. Some of them are complaining about all the beeping on the way here. I join in the tutting and look pointedly at her from number 31 a few times. They seem happy with that.

Before things kick off, we all get a chance to file up and have a look in the box. The people in front of me in the queue are saying that this bit would normally have happened the previous day at the funeral home, but some of the older relatives couldn't do multiple days. They are calling it a 'visitation'. This all sounds very creepy. I'm even more excited now. As we approach the coffin, the people in front are commenting how young she looks, and how happy. Is she even dead? My turn comes and I confirm that she is indeed deceased. I'd like to think I look both younger and happier. As I lean over the body, I place a copy of the film 'Logan's Run' in the casket. This will confuse Baldrick when he digs her up, as she certainly doesn't look thirty.

The priest waffles on for several minutes about number 35's life, making her sound like a pillar of the community. This is all news to me. I certainly never saw her at Neighbourhood Watch. I hold my tongue though. Church isn't a place to be setting the record straight. I know that from bitter experience.

When the time comes for communion, I decide against having one of their meat biscuits after all. I stay sat in my pew and have a chocolate digestive and a cup of tea from my flask instead.

The final hymn is 'All Things Bright and Beautiful', which is a lovely tune, although it's a bit selective about the things it credits God with. Perhaps there's another song about all the things that aren't bright or beautiful, like next door's children. They would probably avoid it for events like this, so as not to depress people.

After the actual burial, which is a bit of a sombre affair, some of the relatives discuss spiritualism as we all walk away from the grave. I ingratiate myself with them by offering some of my sad kitten cards. It just seems the right thing to do. Plans are made to organise an evening with a medium, and as a good friend and neighbour I impress upon them that I definitely want to go to this. They say they want to contact someone called Janet, and I suggest trying to talk to her from number 35 while they're at it. I suspect some of them are a little slow, as they seem slightly confused by this suggestion. It's tentatively arranged for the night after Halloween. I can scarcely contain myself.

***

Before I know it, Halloween has arrived. I'm at Brenda's, and I've just kicked a pumpkin in the face. Brenda's in the kitchen talking about something clever her goddaughter has made that I have to see. When she comes back in, I'm still wiping the pulp off my shoes and she seems to forget what it was she wanted to show me.

We pass the time with a few sherries and a couple of episodes of Autumnwatch. I point out that some eggs have been thrown at Brenda's window. She says it can't have been trick-or-treaters as they are all outside. I tell her not to shoot the messenger as she picks the bits of shell out of the carpet. There's an unaccountable atmosphere for the rest of the evening, which I put down to the spookiness of the occasion.

Things are just as frosty the next morning, when I find I have used up all my toilet rolls on next door's tree the previous night and have to go round and borrow some from them. Begrudging is not the word.

My mood turns back to joy when I remember I'm going to my first seance this evening. I need to make a list of all the questions I want to ask number 35 when she manifests herself. Does she have wings? Is it really all clouds? Or fire? I suppose I shouldn't make assumptions about which way she's gone. Whatever the case, I hope there will be ectoplasm.

***

In the evening, we all assemble in Madam Bucowski's parlour. It looks like it's set up for Bridge. There's a nice big round table in the middle of the room, with a green baize cloth draped over it. There are six of us present, including Madam Bucowski herself, the son Malcolm and his wife, number 35's sister Dolly and her daughter Stephanie, and me. Malcolm has introduced his wife as 'Terry with an eye'. I'm not sure what this means, and can't help but stare. Both eyes seem real enough, which just leaves the question of her having a man's name. The more I look at her, the more nervous she seems. Before I can sensitively make further inquiries, Madam Bucowski stubs out her roll-up, draws the curtains and invites us to be seated.

The first thing she suggests we try is what she calls 'automatic writing'. She says this will help determine the most sensitive members of the group. I can be quite touchy, so I am hopeful of winning this. She gives us each a big piece of paper and a pencil and starts mumbling about us clearing our minds as she lowers the lights, until we are in complete darkness. Then she tells us to allow our hands to write, independently of our minds. There are a lot of scratching sounds and gasps over the next few minutes, until there is finally a faint thud on the far side of the room. Madam Bucowski raises the lights and it becomes clear that my pencil has been thrown some distance by an unknown force. It's sticking out of the forehead of a lady in a portrait over the fireplace. As if that wasn't enough, there is swearing and disturbing imagery all over everyone's paper, except for Terry with the eye's piece, as I couldn't reach that. Madam Bucowski is convinced something primal has been channelled in this room. Dolly says she wants to be sick, but Stephanie calms her. I sneak a look at Terry's hands, which don't seem as large as you might expect.

Madam Bucowski says it's time to try to communicate with whoever is present. She says I may be a kind of lightning rod for the spirits. This is all very exciting. She lowers the lights again, and joins us at the table. We all link hands when instructed, and Madam Bucowski starts moaning. Not in the way a neighbour might, but in the manner of someone who is delirious with flu. It quickly becomes a little annoying, just as a flu sufferer would. She asks if there's anyone there. This is tense stuff. She says to knock once for yes, twice for no. I'm not sure what she's going to do with the information if there are two knocks. Luckily, there is a single quiet tap from somewhere in the vicinity.

Madam Bucowski asks the entity to identify itself. More taps. Five. Ten. Fifteen. We're all counting them off and holding our breath. Twenty. Soon there have been thirty quiet taps.

Now thirty-three.

Thirty-four. Our hearts are in our mouths.

Thirty-five.

Madam Bucowski sighs, rises, turns off the tap in the kitchen properly and returns after a good cough. Dolly is saying 'oh Janet' quite a lot now for some reason. Stephanie is comforting her. Everyone is a little shaken.

Madam Bucowski says she will now attempt to enter a trance state, in order to allow the spirits to talk directly through her, if that is their will. We link hands once more, and she starts moaning like an invalid again. For all I know that's what number 35 sounded like, so I listen intently. Madam Bucowski's voice becomes very deep and raspy. It's very good, although I'm not sure who she's doing. She slowly calls everyone present by name, except me. She says she's fine and not to worry, and not to fight over the money. Could this be number 35? Dolly asks if it's Janet, and Madam Bucowski says it is. She starts saying 'oh Janet' again.

Malcolm asks if she has anyone with her, and Madam Bucowski says there's someone beginning with 'J' or possibly 'B' nearby. He and Dolly look at each other and say 'Uncle Jim' and 'Bernard' simultaneously. Madam Bucowski, still doing her gruff voice, confirms that yes, that's right, it's them. Everyone seems made-up over this.

Madam Bucowski has suddenly become very tired, and indicates that this intense level of communication with the spirit realm takes a great deal out of her. She rolls another cigarette while a satisfied Malcolm settles the bill. As we all get up to leave, Madam Bucowski tells me that something of great strength possesses me. I'm very pleased with this, and thank her very much. She points a bony, yellowed finger at me until I'm in the hallway. I smile and wave goodbye to everyone.

8

REUNITING

A week has gone by since bonfire night, so I've told Brenda it's safe to go back to the unexploded Catherine wheel. Now she's complaining that she can't get the nail out of the coffee table. There's always something.

I took a parcel in for next door this morning because they were out, and when I brought it round this afternoon, I mimed jumping up and down on it. We had a giggle over it on the doorstep, me and her next door. I had a feeling that was the right way to explain what I'd done, and I'm glad she wasn't cross.

This evening is my big school reunion. I'm looking forward to seeing what a mess everyone has made of their lives. Everyone at St. James's Secondary Modern was jealous of how popular I was, so I didn't form many close friends. I hope Tamara and Jumbo will be there. It would be lovely to play another game of *Charlie's Angels*. Tamara was a slight thing, with lank hair and thick glasses. Jumbo struggled with her weight. We all did, poor thing. I was Kelly, Tamara was Sabrina and Jumbo was Jill. Then Jill left the series, so Jumbo wasn't able to play with us for quite a long time, until she agreed to be Kris. It was awkward, as she knew that we had already attempted to cast several other girls in the role by then. Our main enemies at the school were Martha, Shirley and Letitia. They said that *Charlie's Angels* was stupid and Letitia tore my *Look-In* in half once. She said she was the *Bionic Woman*. I hope life has been difficult for her, I really do.

***

I've decided to attend the event in my camouflage jumpsuit. I hope nobody will think I'm trying to hide. I'd have to be stood in front of many leopards to stand a chance of blending into the background in this. As I walk through the playground, the first thing that strikes me is how small everything looks. I could probably run the length of it and back in seconds. I might do, later, but there aren't enough people here to watch me yet. Looking around, though, I see a familiar face coming through the gates. It's Tamara. I don't recognise her straight away, as she's not wearing glasses, but it's her alright, and at least her hair is still lank. I wave her over, excitedly. The closer she gets, the older and more dishevelled she looks. When she reaches me I can see what a huge mistake she has made in wearing black velvet. She has the most dandruff I have ever seen on a person. I don't mention it, of course. Instead, I greet her with a simple 'look at you'. She says how marvellous I look. The best I can do is to say 'look at you' again. I try not to overtly show pity. People don't like that. Without being asked, Tamara starts going on and on about how many children she has, and how old they are. I ask her if she's the old woman who lives in a shoe. She says no, she lives on the estate. She says her partner left her. I'm not surprised. I'm tempted to walk off now, just while she's talking about it. I want to talk about how small the playground is, but she doesn't seem remotely surprised about it. She says she's in playgrounds almost every day. This sounds a bit suspect to me, but then I realise she's just trying to bring the subject back around to all the children she has again. I show an interest in her handbag so she lets me look at it. I ask her how much she would bet that I couldn't throw it right the way across this playground that she doesn't seem to think is amazingly small. She just makes a kind of timid laughing noise, but I do it anyway, and the bag goes clean over the railings. While she heads off to get it, I go into the school.

The assembly hall seems small as well, as does the buffet that has been laid out for us within. I should have eaten before I came out. I have a couple of sausage rolls and start into the plastic cups of red wine that have been left out while I wait for more people to arrive. When Tamara finally comes in she's looking quite flustered. She starts going on about having had to run down several roads after some children who had taken her handbag. That's a disgrace. You can't have anything these days. I'm quite shaken by this story, thinking about how easily that could have been me. To calm down, I have to have another couple of plastic cups of red wine. And one of the white, just to try it. As a result of this, I have to visit the little girls' room.

The little girls' room is unbelievably small. I can barely squeeze into one of the cubicles, and the seat is less than a foot off the ground. Not everything goes in the bowl, but that's not my fault. As I leave I meet someone in the corridor, so I tell them that a child has made a mess. She just says she doesn't work here. Nobody wants to take responsibility for anything any more.

I return to the assembly hall to find that it has filled up a bit in the meantime. There's no sign of Jumbo, but lots of snooty old girls have arrived. To my horror, I see that Tamara is now talking to Shirley and Letitia. I rush over, in case she needs help. She has already had her bag taken once tonight. They back off a bit when I reach them, but pretend to be friendly. Letitia asks how I am, and I make it absolutely clear that I'm fine, and that everything is going just great. You can't show any weakness in this sort of situation.

An old woman comes over with a box of red wine, smiling at us for some reason. Before I can ask where she got it, she's asking us if we'd like a top-up. I nod, and she gestures to all the empty plastic cups on the table and asks which one is mine. They all are, but I just pick up a couple, so as not to appear greedy. Tamara, Shirley and Letitia all seem to have got cups of tea from somewhere, so the old woman just fills my plastic cups and moves on.

I ask Shirley and Letitia what they are doing with themselves these days. I expect to hear the answer 'prostitution', but Shirley works in a building society and Letitia is in human resources at a department store. Initially I think she's going to stop at 'I'm inhuman,' but no. She tells Tamara that actually, she can get her an interview for a part-time position if she wants. I tell her that actually, I would like an interview for a part-time position. She seems surprised and says that she thought I was 'doing great'. She uses her fingers to make it clear that she's quoting me. I say that I am, and ask her if she can get me 'an interview' or not, using the finger trick right back at her. You have to be quite forceful sometimes if you want to get things in this world. She shrugs and says she can. She seems altogether more keen when she turns back to Tamara to ask if she wants to interview for the post too. She says that it sounds like just the sort of thing she's been looking for, as long as she could work her hours around the school runs. Somehow she's brought the conversation back around to her many children again. I point out that there's a speck of something on her shoulder and brush an enormous cloud of dandruff into the air. That seems to stop her. Letitia and Shirley look shocked. I'm not surprised. Tamara's scurf seems to have soured the atmosphere a bit. I try to break the awkward silence by asking Letitia where Martha is tonight. Letitia points out that she *is* Martha. I hope this won't affect my interview.

Later in the evening, I bump into my old headmistress. This is why they tell you not to run in the corridor. They're telling her not to try to get up. Looking down at her, I suggest that she seems a little frail and should consider retiring. She has to shoulder most of the blame for this situation. Someone tells me that she is already retired, and has been for twenty years. I assume she has wandered in here by mistake. They do that sort of thing, sometimes, the old people. There was an old man who used to regularly wander into the playground when I used to go here. At least the headmistress has remembered to dress herself properly. That's a blessing, and I tell her so before I head on to the little

47

girls' room. The wine hasn't agreed with me for some reason. Not much of the sick goes in the bowl, but that's not my fault. As I leave I tell some people in the corridor that a child has made another mess in there. They mumble something about using staff facilities, and not one of them goes in to clean up. That's awful.

***

We're all assembled in the playground in the rain. I can hear lots of the snooty old girls suggesting it was me who set off the fire alarm. It was.

9

WATCHING

I'm at the monthly neighbourhood watch meeting at the community centre. I'm supposed to hand out the newsletters, but they're a bit torn and the ink has run where they've been in the toilet. I'm not sure that they're readable any more, if I'm honest with myself. I might have to say that they were stolen. It's going to be difficult to explain their current condition if I take them in. It was all a bit of a blur after Melissa handed them to me outside. Melissa is our neighbourhood watch coordinator. I could easily have done the job, but they all voted for her, and that's fine. She is quite old, so I'm bound to get another chance soon. On reflection, it was perfectly reasonable of her to ask me to hand out the newsletters, because of her bad leg. She's got a vein.

There's a bicycle parked in the cloakroom, so I stuff the sodden mass of paper into one of the panniers and make my way into the main hall.

There are about twenty of us here tonight, which is an excellent turn-out. Melissa is saying as much, as I sit down. She is full of herself. She is introducing PC Brian May. He is our neighbourhood beat manager. That doesn't mean he manages beatings. He explained that last month, and a few people here seemed to think it was the funniest thing they had ever heard. He tries the line again tonight, but it doesn't go down so well. PC May is looking very smart in his uniform. I often think I would have made a wonderful police officer. Barely a day goes by when I don't run into somebody who I think needs arresting, or wants something confiscated from them. It must be a lovely feeling to be able to just act on those instincts whenever the mood takes you.

Him and her from next door are here. They should get their own house in order before they start coming in here trying to sort the rest of the neighbourhood out. Their garden's a mess, for a start. Maureen and Bernadette are here as well. That's not right. Bernadette's sheltered housing isn't even in the neighbourhood. She's just here for the tea and biscuits. It's tantamount to theft.

PC May says the first order of business is vandalism. He's

listing several places that have been targeted recently. When he mentions the garage doors in the alleyway down the road from me, it sends a shiver down my spine. I did a big drawing on one of those garages only a couple of days ago. I might have only just missed these monsters. It really makes you think.

PC May says that there has been a lot of fly-tipping in the area as well. Him from next door has just turned round and given me a funny look. I don't know what that's about.

After a while, it's question time. Most of the questions are boring. They are about things like gates on alleyways, and burglar alarm advice. When I get my go, I ask PC May when he last used his truncheon. He says they have telescopic batons now. I ask if we can see it, but he says he didn't bring it this evening as he didn't think he'd need it, and smiles. Several people are laughing at this, and Bernadette pipes up to say that's a relief. I'll bet it is, to somebody who is committing fraud just by attending this meeting.

A couple of times during the talk PC May refers to information on the soiled and torn sheets that are currently stuffed in a pannier in the cloakroom. These moments are awkward, as one or two people look around, and there is some murmuring. When PC May has finished wasting his time answering boring security questions, Melissa asks whether everyone has received a copy of the newsletter now. Nobody has. She says 'oh dear' and apologises for a bit. Then her face lights up a little and she asks if she gave them to me to hand out. She's forgotten. I say no, and go on to deny seeing her earlier. Some of the people in the hall look like they don't believe me, which is just typical of the nasty-mindedness I encounter on a daily basis. Melissa says 'oh dear' some more, and PC May suggests that maybe we should stop and have some tea and biscuits now.

During tea and biscuits, Melissa rambles on about distinctly remembering running off all the newsletters on the photocopier at the library. I say that nobody is accusing her of pretending to make the copies and just pocketing the neighbourhood watch funds. It's true, nobody is doing this. Pointing it out only seems to make her more flustered though. PC May consoles Melissa by suggesting to everyone that most of the really vital newsletter information, such as contact details, warnings about cold callers and leaving windows open will have been unchanged from the last newsletter. I offer to drop the newsletter through everyone's letterboxes if she runs some copies off and gives them to me. She says that I'm an absolute rock, and how lovely of me. I wait for PC May to step in and say that what I've offered to do isn't necessary, because of what he *just said*, but he doesn't. This is typical. Now I'm going to have to actually do it. But then something amazing happens. Melissa says that perhaps she's bitten off more than she can chew trying to do everything alone, and that I should become joint coordinator with her. PC May says that this sounds like a very sensible plan. I graciously accept, and there's hardly any murmuring because everybody has heard PC Brian May saying how sensible and fit for the role I am. That's more or less what he has said. He starts going on about meeting up with myself and Melissa once a fortnight, and about disseminating information regularly to the neighbours and lots of other things I probably won't bother doing, but the important thing is that I am now in a position of responsibility.

Now that I can propose policies, I ask PC May whether he thinks we should ban people who don't live in the neighbourhood from these meetings. I don't mention any names, of course, but I'm sure Bernadette shifts awkwardly in her chair. She must have heard me. I practically shouted it. PC May says he thinks the more the merrier, as long as they pay their five pounds a year for membership to cover costs. This is all the justification I need to go over to Maureen and Bernadette, who are helping themselves to their third cup of tea, and the last of the chocolate digestives. I quietly ask if I might see their membership cards. I don't explain why. I don't have to. They know. Surprisingly, they both quite happily reach into their bags. Maureen finds her card first, and it appears valid. Bernadette, however, produces a neighbourhood watch card for her own area. This is it. I have her now. Fraud. But before I can say anything, she apologises and admits that it's the wrong one. She goes on to produce *five more* neighbourhood watch cards, all for different areas, and goes through them carefully until she finds the right one for here, unfortunately valid and up-to-date. She holds it out with a smug smile, returning all the other cards to her bag. She is doing this all over the city, and she knows that I can't touch her for it. All I can do is say 'thank you, ladies' and walk away. They'll keep.

The important thing is that I have become more important this evening. I agree to help Melissa lock up the community centre once the meeting is over, and together we say goodbye to everybody at the door. We wish them all a safe journey home, and watch as PC Brian May rides off on his bicycle.

10

COURTING

I am in the local Magistrate's Court. This is very embarrassing for a joint coordinator of the neighbourhood watch, but at the end of the day Brenda needs to face justice for the incident at Smiths, and I feel that I have to be here to support her. There isn't anybody from the watch here, luckily. If PC Brian May was here, I think I would die of shame. My only excuse is that Brenda doesn't live in my neighbourhood, and thus falls outside my jurisdiction. Brenda has cynically worn the most humble-looking outfit in her wardrobe, but it was raining this morning, so she has spoiled the effect a bit by having a cagoule on with the hood up when we walked into court. It made her look like she was here to do a drive-by shooting. I said as much to an officer outside, but he didn't tackle her. Very lax.

They don't have juries in these places, but I imagine when the judge hears what Brenda has been up to, he'll want to refer the case up to the Crown Court for her to be tried properly. While we're waiting for the judge to show up, Brenda offers me a toffee chew, for which I thank her. I tell her I don't think it's right that she should have one though, in view of what she's done. She says she still doesn't understand how the ink-jet refill got into her pocket in the first place. She claims that she's not even sure what an ink-jet refill is. She promises that she would never deliberately steal anything. Here we are in court, though. Brenda's legal representative is sat on the other side of her. He is called Gordon and he helped Brenda to amicably settle a dispute with her neighbour over a hedge once. He decides not to have a toffee as he may need to talk in a moment. Gordon is balding, but he is compensating for it with a moustache. It's no compensation at all, though, as it just looks like he has combed down some very long nostril hairs. I don't say anything, of course.

The judge has walked in. This is amazing. It's Miss Parker, my old geography teacher in secondary school. I had no idea she had this sort of power. She once gave me a detention for wearing earrings in class. Brenda is going down for sure. Now two more judges have walked in. They are taking this really seriously if it needs three judges. Poor Brenda. Her chickens are all coming home to roost.

Gordon enters a plea of guilty, on the grounds that his client wishes the matter to be brought to a conclusion as swiftly as possible. He asks that their honours take into account the mitigating circumstance that his client did not plan the crime with malice aforethought, and that in fact his client has no memory of putting the ink-jet refill cartridge in her pocket.

I want to act up, but there's no blackboard, so Miss Parker doesn't turn her back at any point. It's an open and shut case, and it's all over in about ten minutes. Miss Parker speaks for the three judges. She says that they have decided to give Brenda twenty hours community service as her punishment. She says that the court has been lenient because this is a first offence. Brenda is now officially guilty of theft, despite what she said to me earlier. So that makes her a liar as well. The ten commandments seem to mean nothing to her. Who knows what else she's done? I feel like I barely know her at the moment. In time, I know I will forgive her for what she has done though, because it's the right thing to do, and the fact that she won't be in prison for Christmas is cause for celebration. Sadly, I only have time to let off a couple of party poppers before the bailiff confiscates the box. I hope Brenda understands that those will have to be replaced.

Now that I've seen some justices of the peace in action, I would like to become one. It seems a natural progression from joint coordinator of the neighbourhood watch. Miss Parker wants us to clear the court for another case, but before we do, I put my hand up and shout 'Miss' until she answers me. I tell her about my current position of power, and that I am very interested in judging people, and ask her how she got started. She says she began when she was still teaching, as it enabled her to keep in touch with the children when they left school. She says that there is an application process with interviews, but that if I am serious, there is probably no reason why I couldn't volunteer. I pick her up on the word 'volunteer', and she explains that it is an unpaid post, although some expenses can be claimed. I tell her that I see, and wink. She pretends not to understand, but we both know what that's all about. You can tell. I ask her about qualifications, as I have several O-Levels, but she says that there are no formal qualifications required to be a magistrate and that there are some forms and leaflets I could look at in the front office. This is incredible. I ask whether I will be able to arrest people, and she laughs and tells me that I already have the power to make a citizen's arrest. All the pieces are falling into place. It's only a matter of time now before I put Maureen and Bernadette behind bars, where they belong. I tell Miss that I have no further questions, your honour.

11

JOBSEEKING

Today is my interview at the department store where Martha works. I have power-dressed for the occasion in my best tweed twin-set. It's like one Michelle Obama wore once, and it screams timeless elegance, according to the catalogue. They'll have to sit up and take notice when they see me in my screaming business-wear. As I enter the store, the first thing that greets me is the perfume counter. There's a girl there spraying people with various scents. That's a wonderful job. I hope I get to do that. I can already think of ways to do it better than the way she's doing it. She's not even hiding.

My interview is on the top floor. I don't want to be late, but once I'm in the lift with all those people I can't help but press every single button. There are two basements, but we only get a brief glimpse of them as the door doesn't stay open very long when nobody gets out. I press their buttons again, but it looks like we're going to have to go all the way up before we can come back down again. There's a lot of tutting going on behind me. They're clearly disappointed too. The second time I reach the top floor I check my watch and realise that I should probably get out. It doesn't do to keep people waiting for too long. I go over to see Martha. She's sat looking out of a little window like a bookie. I waved at her from the lift the first time I got to the top floor, but she just looked puzzled. I hope she hasn't forgotten about me. I remind her that I'm here for my job, and she directs me to a small seating area down the corridor. Tamara is here. She is dressed very smartly, but her and the black leatherette seating around her are covered in scurf. I'm convinced her head must be shrinking from all this skin loss. Another woman is also here, and she is wearing the other outfit Michelle Obama wears from the catalogue. It is ten pounds cheaper, and frankly it looks it. They'll see right through her. I don't say anything, of course. I just smile politely. Tamara starts going on and on about what a rush it was this morning to get all her many children to whatever institutions they are all kept at during the day. I don't need this. I have to prepare for my interview. Now the other woman is chiming in about how difficult it is to organise child care. Her name is Helen and she says that she has a case of the terrible twos. I point her to a toilet sign I saw on the way down the corridor. She doesn't go though. Instead she bangs on about her toddler Cilla being a handful. Helen appears to be dandruff-free, but she has a shocking array of spots on her chin. It's like a big red beard. Surely they won't let her spray perfume at the general public downstairs looking like that. Tamara asks me if I think I'm well-prepared. She says she isn't, because of her many children. I don't really know what she means, but I tell her that I am very well prepared indeed. She can't prove otherwise. This seems to make her more nervous. She runs a hand through her hair and emits a flurry of scurf that twinkles in the shaft of sunlight coming through the window.

Helen is looking at her curriculum vitae. I ask her how many O-Levels she has. I know for a fact that I have two more than Tamara. Helen smiles and says she can barely remember her GCSE results, but that she's hoping her degree in marketing will help. Her O-Levels must be poor if she's pretending not to be able to remember them. A smart young man in a tank top and pin striped trousers emerges from a door at the end of the seating area and invites Helen to come through now please. Tamara wishes her good luck. I don't, because I don't.

Myself and Tamara fill the next quarter of an hour reminiscing. Apparently Jumbo is in New Zealand now. Tamara says she went on a jet. A jumbo jet. She seems to think this is really funny. It's nervous laughter, I suppose, but she's practically in tears with it. She's hysterical. I'm considering striking her when Helen comes back out, smiling smugly. Tamara recovers a little and asks her how it went, and she says that she thinks it was alright. That can't be true. Then the smart young man appears again and it's my turn. I follow him through the door into a little office. He joins a middle-aged woman behind a desk and invites me to sit the other side. The woman apologises for keeping me, but that they are running late. She is called Celeste and the young man is James. Celeste is wearing a quite formal charcoal business suit. It's not something Michelle Obama would wear. Not in the catalogue, anyway. She wants to know what I think I could bring to the exciting world of retail. I tell her I'm good with numbers. I am. I don't forget how many O-Levels I have, for a start. I tell her I have people skills. Brenda always says I could easily have more friends if something or other. So that's true as well. My retail experience is mainly on the other side of the counter, but I suggest that perhaps that gives me a unique insight into what the customer really wants. James interrupts, saying that perhaps it isn't all that unique. I tell him we'll have to agree to disagree. He smiles and asks me what I think my biggest weakness is. I don't want to tell the truth this time. Anyone would be stupid to volunteer information about their weaknesses, as they can then be used against them. I say I'm too much of a perfectionist. Celeste asks me what I think my biggest strength is. I say it's a toss-up between loyalty and long-distance throwing. And I don't have children. Celeste tells me that they don't discriminate against families. I say that I don't want to tell them how to run their business. She asks me where I see myself in five years, and I say in her chair. She smiles at this. I'm happy that she doesn't take it as the threat it so obviously is. James is looking at my curriculum vitae now. I hope he's counting those O-Levels. He says there's a bit of a gap in my employment record. I say I've been taking time out for self-improvement. He doesn't press me on this. At first, I consider this a blessing, but then I begin to wonder if he has made assumptions about how much improvement I've had to make. I haven't been bravely overcoming a learning disability or something. I really hope he's looked at those O-Levels now. Celeste interrupts my train of thought to ask me if there's anything that I'd like to ask them. I wonder if they can tell me a little about the job. Celeste turns to James, who says that it's largely basic admin work. He probably says more, as he goes on for about five minutes. I wait patiently for him to finish and ask if

I'll ever get to spray perfume at people. He smiles and says it's all hands on deck here and he supposes anything is possible. There's nothing else I need to know. Celeste hands me a piece of paper. It's just a short psychometric test, she says, nothing too taxing. She tells me there's a little room just down the corridor I can pop into to fill it out and they both thank me very much for coming in.

Later in the afternoon, I phone Martha to see if she has any insight into how I've got on. She says she's overheard Celeste and James saying that they've never seen anything like what I've done on my psychometric test and all over the desk. I'm quietly confident.

12

SERVICING

It's a lovely sunny day, so I've come out to watch Brenda doing her community service. They've got her picking up litter along the dual carriageway this morning. They've made her wear a high-visibility orange jumpsuit that makes her look like a political prisoner. She isn't one, though. She's a convicted thief. Brenda isn't the victim of some faceless bureaucratic machine. She is merely hostage to her own broken moral compass. She sees ink-jet refills and thinks to herself that she has some kind of God-given right to have them, and that society can just go hang. It's criminality, pure and simple, and it's good to see her paying her dues here.

For the morning shift, she has been teamed up with a teenager called Laurence. He says he is probably better known for his graffiti art, but that he can't reveal his tag name to me. I tell him that I recently did a large drawing of a man's private thing on a garage door around the corner from my house, and somebody had come along and done some graffiti on that and ruined it, so I thought it was right that he was paying for his crime. Laurence says he thinks he has seen my work around town and presents his fist for bumping. I meet it with mine, and he mumbles something about respect. It's good that a young man respects his elders, but I hope this doesn't mean I'm in a gang now. I have too many demands on my time as it is.

Brenda is complaining about her back from bending over to get bottles and picking up fly-tipped bin bags. I would like to help, but then what lesson would she be learning? None, that's what. Before Brenda started her sentence, I told her that she needed to hit the largest person she could see, in order to try to become top dog. I know all about this from watching the Australian reality show *Prisoner Cell Block H*. Laurence doesn't have a mark on him, so I don't know who Brenda can have punched. It's possible that there were three people on her chain gang at the start of the day, perhaps more. There are a lot of bushes along this dual carriageway where she might have hidden a body. Perhaps she has only allowed Laurence to tag along as her 'bitch'. I was only suggesting a light demonstrative punishment beating to establish her dominance. What has she become? I tentatively ask her how her morning has been, and she replies that everybody has been very nice. If all the other criminals are being 'very nice' to her, I can only imagine the brutal and vicious assault she has made them watch. Then she says that the worst part of the job is dealing with road kill. This sends a shiver down my spine. Poor Laurence. What awful things might Brenda have made him do this morning? And it's only half past ten. I tell Brenda that she was only supposed to punch them. She says no, they have to scrape them off the road and bag them up for the incinerator. Laurence says I am hardcore. I don't know what this means. I suppose I should be happy that Brenda at least has a plan to deal with what she has done. It's best that I don't know too much more about the details.

Brenda and Laurence have been provided with a fluorescent green friendly-looking electric utility vehicle in which to collect all the rubbish they find by the roadside. Every so often, Laurence gets in and moves it a hundred yards further up the dual carriageway. I take the opportunity to pop home and fetch a bin-liner's worth of old shoes and a portable television that doesn't work any more since we went digital, and sling these into the back of their electric pick-up truck. I can't abide fly-tipping, so this feels like I'm doing my bit for both the community and the environment. I point out to Brenda that her old sofa would just about fit in the back of their vehicle. She insists that she doesn't have an old sofa. This is a bone of contention between us. I've spoken to the council about Brenda's old sofa before, but they said they couldn't do a thing about it while the offending furniture was still in her living room. I don't labour the point today, as she has other things on her mind, and I don't want to end up in a series of bags on the back of her truck myself.

I tell them both that I'll be back tomorrow. I will, too. I have about fifty VHS tapes and a broken bird table to get rid of. Before I leave, I make Laurence promise not to let Brenda talk him into going ram-raiding in their truck. He still has his whole life ahead of him.

13

SIBLING

B renda's sister Beryl has arrived to stay for the weekend. We collected her from the station and all the way back in the car she kept winking at me and whispering 'what are you going to do to her next, eh?'. Brenda went in ahead of us to switch off the house alarm. While we were waiting in the porch, Beryl shouted over the klaxon that Brenda had told her about some of the pranks I had been playing. She gave me a 'two thumbs up' sign. I told her I didn't know what she was talking about.

Eventually, Brenda worked out how to silence the alarm, and we settled into the living room for a lovely cup of coffee. Brenda has moved the sofa to cover up the writing I did in her carpet with the lady shaver. As a consequence, we have to sit very close to the telly indeed now, and Kerrang is quite loud, so Beryl turns it off after a few minutes. Our ears are ringing. Brenda says she now has a universal remote control, but she can't program it without the original one that got run over. I've suggested she buys a second universal remote to program the first one, and she seems satisfied with this solution.

When Brenda leaves to go to the little girls' room, Beryl winks at me and suggests we 'do her a favour' and pull down her 'appalling' curtains. I am shocked at this suggestion, although the curtains are indeed appalling. Also, the nets are filthy and have what looks like dried egg on them.

When Brenda returns, the conversation turns to the two sisters' young life growing up in Dudley. Beryl continually refers to Brenda as 'Daddy's little favourite'. Beryl is the senior of the two by five years. She looks ten years older and dresses twenty years younger. She is wearing a lot of make-up. She looks like a poorly decorated cake. If she took all that slap off, her head would probably be half the size. I don't say anything, of course. It's not my place.

Beryl teases Brenda about her 'ruddy complexion'. There's just no need for that sort of language. Perhaps about her hair, but not her complexion. As soon as I've pointed this out though, I realise that I've done more harm than good. I've just encouraged Beryl. She says she likes Brenda's hair, but then completely reverses it by asking her if the gardener charges extra for it. Poor Brenda. I can't let this continue, so quick as a flash, I kick the coffee table over. Time seems to slow down momentarily, and I can hear the thud, thud, thud of the cupcakes hitting the carpet, and the grinding metallic sound of the tray rolling around the cafetière. That comes to a halt, and all is silence, broken only by me having a quick slurp from my mug, which I am lucky enough to have been holding on to. And then Beryl bursts out laughing. I don't know what more I can do to help Brenda here. Her sister is simply an awful person.

As Brenda starts to mop things up, Beryl raises her palm to me. For her sake, this had better not be the physical attack it's looking like. But no, she's saying 'high five'. It's some sort of congratulation. I want to tell her how unpleasant I think she is being, but she is Brenda's house guest, so it isn't my place. I slap her palm, but only because it would be rude to leave her hanging. That's just not the way I was raised. I can see from Brenda's expression that she isn't happy with any of this. It's a difficult situation. I would offer to help Brenda clean up, but that would mean both of us being down on our knees while Beryl sits there like the queen of the universe. That wouldn't do at all.

To try to break the uncomfortable silence that is developing, I ask Beryl what she does for a living. By the time I've finished my coffee I realise she's still talking. I think she started off by going on about some government scheme to make families more self-important. I only really listened to the first couple of words, as that's long enough for most people to say what they do. Some people have careers shorter than Beryl's job description. I try to stop her by saying that it all sounds very interesting, but that's a gamble that doesn't pay off. She's launching into anecdotes now. I try putting Kerrang back on, and this seems to drown her out. I keep watch out of the corner of my eye, and when I'm fairly certain that her mouth has stopped moving, I turn it off again.

Brenda rights the table, disposes of quite a few brown-looking kitchen towels and sits down to join us once more. Thinking back on the last few minutes, I probably should have turned the telly on first, rather than going straight for the coffee table. There's no point dwelling on these things though. You live, you learn, and you move on. I ask what the plan is for tomorrow. Beryl says that Brenda has promised to take her to Dudley zoo, as she hasn't been there since she was a child. I suggest that they're probably still looking for her. She laughs and says that I am awful. I say that no, she is awful, and I mean it.

***

The following morning, Brenda and Beryl pick me up as I have insisted. This is partly because I don't want Beryl picking on Brenda all day, but mainly because I have never been to Dudley zoo. There are bears, and Beryl says that I should throw Brenda's duffel coat to them to see if they look any more like Paddington wearing it than she does. That's how much of the conversation in the car goes, with her suggesting that various elements of Brenda's ensemble, or her compact disc collection, should be hurled at apes or out of the window, or that Beryl herself should be fed to something. On a more interesting note, Beryl says that Dudley zoo has the largest collection of Tectons in the world. When I ask how many that is, she says twelve. Twelve Tectons. Brenda confirms that it's true. Twelve of them. And they're big. I don't know what Tectons are, but I'm excited. I'm picturing armoured mammoths. When we arrive at the zoo, and go through the turnstile gates with the word ZOO written on them in enormous letters, and the Tectons turn out just to be some curvy buildings, I'm furious.

One of the animals is simply labelled 'Geoffroy's Cat' and appears to be a tabby. I assume Geoffroy is one of the keepers here. I quite like the penguins, but my favourite bit is the Lemur enclosure. They are inquisitive and excitable, like me. A member of staff gives us an informative talk about them. Then I take him to one side and quietly tell him that Beryl has been trying to touch a Mongoose Lemur in an inappropriate way. He says that members of the public aren't allowed to touch the Lemurs in any way, and asks her to leave the enclosure. He handles it professionally, so there isn't as much of a scene as I would have liked, but it's enough to make Brenda snigger. That's normally a trait I would frown upon, but today it makes me happy.

The zoo is very hilly, with a big ruined castle at the top. The curvy buildings are staggered around it. Some of them are better than others. There's one called the Birdhouse, but there aren't any birds in it. They've just filled it with children. There are plenty of those in Coventry, if I wanted to see them, which I don't. Beryl stares at the child enclosure for a while, though, just like she stared at the baby orang utan. She mumbles something about feeling more and more broody lately, since she's been working with the self-absorbed families, or whatever it is.

Myself and Brenda eventually persuade Beryl to move on, and we go to something called the Polar Bear Complex. I'm not sure if it's named after the animal or some kind of mental condition, as there are no polar bears. It's an impressively deep pit, though, which is always a good thing. Beryl stares into this for ages too. She is so maudlin today, it seems almost wrong to throw any of her belongings into this big empty concreted hole. Moments later the three of us are staring down at the red speck that is Beryl's bag. I will admit that I initially mistook this moment for quiet contemplation, and appreciation of a job well done. With twenty-twenty hindsight though, everyone is agreed that this was at the very least avoidable. Beryl's first thought on the matter is that her shoes are in that bag. Looking down, we can see that she is indeed barefoot. This seems odd to me, and I say as much, but Beryl is of the opinion that grabbing somebody's handbag while they are having a bit of a think and hurling it into a large concrete pit is in some way more odd. Now she has a problem with the way I went about it, as well. She's ranting about the fact that I just did it, without laughing, without saying anything, without even changing my facial expression. She says that I want locking up. Then that reminds her that her keys are in the bag as well, along with her money, and her phone, and her cards. Cards. I don't have any of my sad kitten cards with me. I'm being called a lunatic by this dreadful, child-crazy woman, and I'm not sure how best to handle this unpleasant situation. Then Brenda grabs Beryl by the arm and tells her that they'll go and find a member of staff, that they'll be able to retrieve the bag. She assures her that this sort of thing must happen all the time. She pauses for a moment and then asserts that this sort of thing *does* happen all the time, rolling her eyes at me as she walks Beryl away down the steps.

Less than fifteen minutes later, Beryl is back in possession of her bag, and a keeper, possibly Geoffroy himself, is telling her that this sort of thing does indeed happen all the time. He advises her to try to keep a tighter grip on her bag from now on, and laughs. The way Brenda has taken charge of the situation has had a profound effect on Beryl. For the rest of the day, she is actually pleasant to Brenda, and she doesn't try to persuade me to play tricks on her any more either. She also elects to wear shoes like a normal person.

All the way back in the car, Brenda and Beryl reminisce, but it's not like yesterday. Now they are wistful, discussing happy shared memories and laughing. It's very boring and non-inclusive for me though, so I mainly just look out of the window and make gestures at other road users. When she drops me back at my house, Brenda makes me wait at my gate for a moment. She goes to the boot and hands me a brown paper bag containing a furry stuffed toy Lemur that she has secretly purchased at the gift shop. She says it's just to say thank you. It's hard to work people out sometimes. I wave the sisters off, push over next door's bird table and head inside to name my new Lemur.

14

STALKING

I am on a stake-out. I'm at the neighbourhood watch meeting in a sports hall. This isn't my area, although I played badminton here a couple of times as a child. I hope nobody asks me for a membership card, because I don't have one. I'm sitting quietly at the back, drinking tea and having a few biscuits while listening to the opening remarks. A door creaks behind me and they're here. My quarry, Maureen and Bernadette, have arrived. I look daggers at them as they tip-toe over to the refreshment table, their shoes squeaking on the floor surface with every step. It's a disgrace. They are brazenly helping themselves to tea and biscuits at a neighbourhood watch meeting in someone else's neighbourhood. I balance my cup and saucer and my remaining biscuits on my lap so that I can take some incriminating photographs on my mobile phone. The biscuits here are better than the ones at our neighbourhood watch. They have Bourbons, custard creams, Nice biscuits and chocolate fingers. I think Hobnobs are my favourite, but the bits stick in my teeth, so it's probably for the best that they don't have those here. Chocolate fingers come a close second. They are very moreish. I've lost count of how many I've had this evening. It's easy to see why Maureen and Bernadette pursue this life of fraud and deceit, pretending to be from various neighbourhoods. It doesn't make it right, though. I get a good shot of Bernadette pouring two teas, and another of her passing a cup to Maureen. With the third, I zoom out a little for an establishing shot, taking in some of the surroundings as well as the pair of them loading a side plate with biscuits and cupcakes. I hadn't even seen the cakes earlier. While the two criminals are sitting down, I go back over to the refreshment table and select a few of the cakes, pouring myself another tea while I'm there. I notice they've taken the last of the chocolate fingers. I know, because I had left three on that plate. They really are something else. Not a thought for other people.

While I'm eating all the cakes, I begin to wonder exactly what our five pounds a year membership fee has been going towards. Even the tea is better here. I will have to discuss this with PC

Brian May, although the last time I saw him there was a furry mould growing on one of his panniers. It's hard to know how much stock to put in his opinions any more, when the man lets his bicycle get into that sort of a condition.

The watch coordinator here is a young bespectacled man called Mandeep. He's introducing their police liaison officer, a WPC called Madhulata. She is their equivalent of PC Brian May, but she likes to keep things less formal than he does. It seems a little inappropriate, but that's her business. She's mainly talking about graffiti and shoplifting. She's very happy to say that an alleyway nearby has been fenced off since the last meeting, and that crime levels have dropped as a result, apart from graffiti, which has gone up because of the new fence to draw on. At the next meeting, they are going to have an expert on burglar alarms come to give a talk. I make a note of the name, so that I can get them to come and see us as well, or preferably instead. Eventually, the main business is over and Mandeep points us all toward the refreshment table, telling us to enjoy what he says is an excellent biscuit and cake selection provided gratis by Malik's Provisions around the corner. When we rush over, most of the plates are empty, though, except for the Bourbons, and those are my least favourite of the ones they had. This is a shambles. Some of the people are looking at me, presumably because they can tell from my bearing and the lapel badge I made myself that I am a watch coordinator. I probably should have removed the lapel badge, given that I am undercover. All I can do here is nod in the direction of Bernadette and Maureen and tut loudly. Then I remember my phone. I beckon Mandeep over and introduce myself, showing him my lapel badge. He shakes my hand, and says what a wonderful idea it is for the different watch groups to interact. I show him the shot of Bernadette and Maureen loading their plates and ask him whether this is sufficient evidence for WPC Madhulata to arrest them, or for us to make a citizen's arrest. He just laughs and says that he is thinking of getting one of these phones too. Justice is just a joke to Mandeep, it would seem. Over his shoulder, I can see Bernadette and Maureen waving at me. There's no point even telling Mandeep that they aren't from around here, as he seems to think that's a good thing. They've won this round. I could spit, I really could. But I might hit WPC Madhulata. The best I can manage is showing them the finger with my left hand while I'm shaking hands with Mandeep. He's promising to come to our next meeting. I'm not sure how welcome his cavalier attitude to the law will be with our little group, but all I can do is be polite in the circumstances. Being a better person than Bernadette or Maureen is at least a victory of sorts.

15

CELEBRATING

I am at a do. My niece and her beau have decided to delay formally announcing their engagement until the ring has passed through my digestive tract. I hadn't really thought about the whole business of getting it back. I'm not sure what all the fuss is about anyway. If Susan was going to be so precious about it, she shouldn't have been taking it off to show people the deeply personal and meaningful inscription. She is right up herself. The beau appears to be some kind of rugby player type, with a neck thicker than his head. I haven't caught his name so far, but I imagine it'll all be called off long before I would ever need to use it.

They've put on quite a nice buffet, I'll give them that. I must have had ten vol-au-vents already. I suppose this is all just more that I'll have to sort through tomorrow, but I'm trying not to let that spoil my evening. The event is being held in a function room at a sports ground. There are quite a few thick-necked men milling around what's-his-name. They all have very big, booming laughs. I imagine they're being told about the ring. The inscription on the inside of the band was 'You complete me'. I don't know what that's supposed to mean, unless they just ran out of letters. You complete mess? You complete mental? Either would make more sense where Susan is concerned. It's hard to enjoy this plate of sausage rolls knowing that she's just across the room looking daggers at me, it really is.

My sister comes over with her husband just as I'm trying to tuck into the salmon and broccoli quiche. He seems happy enough, but then it isn't an open bar, so he hasn't been hit with a large bill for any of this fiasco yet. The few bottles of cheap champagne that they made such a play of pouring out in a fountain earlier on certainly aren't going to break the bank. Margaret makes a remark about me seeming to be enjoying the finger food. Before I know what has happened, I've raised my middle finger and told her to 'feast on that'. I feel a little bit bad about this. In some ways, she is an innocent victim here. She forces a peculiar laugh for the benefit of the other people in the vicinity. They are presumably friends and neighbours, but I don't recognise any of them. It seems best to proceed as if nothing has happened, so in my most demure voice, I tell Margaret that yes, this is a lovely spread. The tiny sandwiches are hardening and curling a bit, but I don't say anything about that. I'm not that sort of person. I'd like to follow up by complementing Margaret on how lovely she looks this evening, but I don't want to sound insincere. Also, it's entirely possible that someone is forcing her to wear that outfit. Whatever the case, I'm quite sure that the last thing she would want me to do is remind her about it. David, her husband, is still smiling, putting on a brave face, but you can see a haunted despair in his eyes when you get up close. He was a vital young man before Susan came along. She has drained them both. She is something else.

I ask Margaret what the colour of her hair is called. She says that it is her natural colour. I suppose it might have been, once. I don't really remember. At least David has had the good grace to just go grey, along with his hair. Margaret is only fooling herself. I tell them that this is probably the best engagement party this club has ever thrown for Susan, and they both agree. Margaret says that she has a good feeling about this one though, that he's a keeper. Because I'm trying to listen out for his name, I note with some frustration that she refers to him as 'this one' throughout our conversation. It seems likely that Margaret doesn't know what he's called either.

After we have exchanged niceties for what seems like an eternity, Susan and what's-his-name wander over to join us. What's-his-name calls them by their first names, which I find a bit forward. He just nods at me solemnly, which I think is more appropriate given that he is a complete stranger. David playfully punches him on the shoulder and says 'ah, this one'. This is just embarrassing. I wonder if even Susan knows what his name is.

What's-his-name makes a joke about only having the ten pints this evening as he has to go to training in the morning. I ask if he means rugby or toilet. He says rugby, and goes into excruciating detail about what is involved. I get through it by nodding and having a few pieces of the quiche, which is actually very nice. When it seems like he's nearly finished talking, I tell him that's all very interesting. But I stare at him with my eyes crossed while I'm saying it and then leave my mouth hanging open, so that he knows I don't really mean it. He must know. He looks unsure of himself, and then nods over at his rugby friends, who are now doing a chant of some kind. He makes some excuse about needing to make sure that 'those buggers don't die of thirst' and slopes off. I make a hand gesture behind his back and then turn to Susan, closing my mouth and uncrossing my eyes as I do so. I tell her that he is probably my favourite of all her fiancés, and I honestly do mean that.

16

LISTING

My niece has decided to have her wedding list at the very same department store at which I hope soon to be working, although they haven't officially confirmed anything yet. When I heard about this coincidence, I just had to come and help Susan with putting the list together. I feel more invested in this one than any of Susan's previous engagements. In a way, I feel like I gave birth to the ring she's wearing. She insists that she never wants to see the video I made of that on my phone though. We have a special two hour appointment to wander around the store and choose things. The beau isn't here. Susan says she had barely told him that I'd be tagging along with them when he announced that he would be getting called away to an important meeting. He said he trusts Susan's judgement completely, apparently. It's a shame he's not joining us, because I still haven't caught his name. It's probably not important though. He sounds the flighty type, so this could all be called off at any moment. And I doubt he's ever had an important meeting in his life.

Susan is talking to Judith. Judith is our expert wedding advisor. I might run into her on this floor sometimes if they let me spray perfume at the customers. Judith has given us an easy-to-use scanner with which we can add things to the list as we walk round the store. All we have to do is point it at the bar codes and change the quantity if need be. I'm in charge of the scanner while Susan is with Judith. I explained to Judith that I can operate a mobile phone while I was wrestling it out of her hands. I've been looking through the small selection of DVDs they have here. There are forty copies of The Exorcist on the list now, if people want to buy that for the happy couple.

Finally, my niece comes over with Judith, who is smiling smugly. She is right up herself, you can tell. As soon as you put 'expert' in somebody's job title, they think they're Stephen Hawking. I ask Judith, out of interest, how many times she has been married. Judith tells us that she and someone called Justin are planning to wed for the first and only time next year. This makes her at best ill-informed, and at worst a fraud, in my book. However, my niece seems perfectly happy with this as an answer, and congratulates Judith, so I don't say anything. Judith asks me if I'm happy with all the features on the scanner. I tell her yes, I'm more than capable of operating it. She's running through all the features again, and every so often she looks at the scanner. You can tell she wants to play with it herself, but I'm in charge of it now. She says that we should keep an eye on the running total on the LCD screen, so that we can stick approximately to the two and a half thousand pound mark that she says is appropriate for the number of guests Susan and what's-his-name are planning to invite. The total is saying less than four hundred pounds at the moment, so that leaves plenty. Judith says that we should aim to have two or three gifts on the list per guest. That is typical of Susan's greed. She is something else, she really is. It's Margaret's fault of course, for spoiling her all these years. I don't say anything, but she'll be getting one gift from me and she can like it or lump it.

Judith reminds us about the key classic wedding list items we should be considering on our way round the store, such as cookware, dinnerware, toasters, coffee machines, lamps, vases and duvet sets. She reels off some expensive-sounding brand names. She says we should definitely consider asking for a full set of china as well. Then she tells us to enjoy ourselves, and to just bring the scanner back to her when we're done, and that we know where to find her if we need her. The so-called expert flim-flam woman wanders back to her area, and we're finally free to explore.

Susan is looking at a coffee machine that costs as much as a telly. I've never even seen her drink coffee, but she says that's because she didn't have a coffee machine. I have to admit that it's well-built. It takes quite a lot of force to snap one of the nozzles off the display model, and even then, there's a spare. Susan insists that this machine is an integral part of her dream kitchen, and so I scan it.

We look at china patterns for what seems like an eternity. Susan is initially very taken with a plain white set entitled 'Innocence', but she's put off a bit by my laughter. We get into a bit of a heated debate over the relative merits of Wedgwood and Royal Doulton. To my mind, it stands to reason that anything with 'Royal' in the name is going to be better, but she won't be told. She is so stubborn, just like her mother. She needs to learn that she can't have her own way all the time. I should get to make at least half of these decisions. Just to put an end to the argument, I pretend to scan the banded Wedgwood set. As we are moving on toward the kitchenware, I try to surreptitiously scan the lovely

Royal Doulton set with the lace motif. Unfortunately, as I check the screen on the scanner, I realise that I've accidentally scanned a different box containing a novelty set featuring a modern take on the classic willow pattern. It has a large, colourful, cartoon design of a big-toothed rural Chinese labourer in a pointy hat. If I had to describe it in one word, it would be 'racist'. If Susan had just listened to me in the first place, this would never have happened. It's entirely her fault. I hope she and what's-his-name enjoy their racist china, I really do.

Susan tells me to scan a particularly expensive set of pots and pans bearing the signature of some French chef or other. I try to tell her that she's just paying for the name, but she's not having any of it. Susan explains that mummy and daddy have promised her a cooker with six hobs, so she needs lots of nice things to put on them. As she eyes a collection of casserole dishes from the same chef, I point out that I've never seen her cook anything in her life. She would be better off asking for pizza vouchers. You can't tell her anything, though. She should be choosing all these things on the basis of what they're going to look like covered in dust and cobwebs. I'll admit that the ceramic casserole set will probably still look quite nice after a few years on a high shelf. Perhaps these things will be heirlooms, of sorts.

We venture into toiletries, as Susan thinks that a big basket of assorted soaps, moisturisers and bath salts should definitely be somewhere on the list. Encouraging her beau to wash is probably a good idea, to be fair. Susan herself should avoid soap though, as it will lift the orange out of her face. I don't really see where a basket is going to fit in her bathroom anyway. She'd have to get a special little table to put it on. Moments later, she has made me scan a special little table to put it on. There is a nest of them just on the corner of the soap basket display. That's how they get you.

While we are in toiletries, I spy the perfume woman idling about. This is unacceptable. We are customers, and she hasn't even attempted to creep up on us. I will probably report her in due course, but for now I go over to introduce myself, as a potential colleague. When I point out that we may soon be working together, she looks me up and down and says 'right' very slowly before smiling and introducing herself. Her name is Justine and she is working her way through a degree in Media Studies. This explains a lot. She's not serious about her profession at all. I ask her how much perfume she has actually sold here, and she says that isn't exactly how it works, as she is a beauty consultant. She does makeovers, and helps people to appreciate the full range of available products. She imagines that she has indirectly sold a lot, though. In fact, she seems to think that her contribution to the overall shopping experience has probably indirectly lead people to purchase sofas and fridges. Unless she's actually drugging the customers, I can't really see it. On the one hand, it's encouraging to hear the job satisfaction in what she's saying, but on the other hand, Justine is clearly a right little madam. When they make me her counter manager, I can see that I will have to bring her down a peg or two. She still hasn't sprayed anything at me, so I pick up a bottle from the counter myself. It appears to be called 'Circus'. This is bringing to mind a clown's insoles and animal droppings for me, but Justine says it's a really fresh mix of flowers with hints of toffee apple and candy floss. She suggests that it might be a little young for me. She makes quotation marks with her fingers in the air to make it seem like someone else has said this about me, but I've just heard it from her lips. I depress the nozzle.

Justine is down, clutching her face. I realise that I had the bottle pointed the wrong way, and I'm glad of it now, if that's what it's like. As I'm leaning over to ask if she's alright, I get a whiff of 'Circus', and I must confess that she was right about it being a little young for me. Justine smells like a child's birthday party. I wouldn't wish this on my worst enemy. She says she'll be OK, but that she'll have to leave her post for a moment. With that, she's off in the general direction of a door marked 'STAFF ONLY'. I can't wait until I'm allowed through that door.

Susan calls me over to scan a pair of matching table lamps, and a pair of matching tables to put them on. Then we head for the lift, as she wants to visit the bedroom department next. Susan is utterly unimpressed by the two basements and refuses to get out at either one. I will never understand her. Two basements. There could be anything down there. I ask her if department stores have morgues, for example, but she won't even entertain the idea. It's like we're not related at all. I don't press the top floor button this time. It's tempting to go up quickly and wave at Martha, but that might seem unprofessional if James or Celeste saw me. Also, at the end of the day, until I actually have the job and Martha and I become work friends and regular lunchtime companions, she is still my enemy for what she drew on my pull-out poster of Bosley. Tamara, Jumbo and I didn't have anyone to play Bosley when we were being Charlie's Angels, so that poster of him leaning against his desk with his arms folded, next to Charlie's loudspeaker, was all we had. And Martha drew that awful thing on him. It was very distracting when we were pretending he was giving us our missions. Jumbo couldn't look at it at all. I can't help but wonder about the effect it may have had on Tamara. It was just terrible, what Martha did. Or it might have been Letitia.

We leave the lift and walk into the bedroom department. I will never stop being impressed by lifts. Every time the door opens, you're somewhere else. It's like Doctor Who. In this episode, we have materialised on the planet of the beds.

As we are walking among the beds to get to the shelving containing all the duvet sets, I notice that one of the customers in here has brought a child with her. If I see an assistant, I will point this out, as it will probably try to jump up and down on the beds. Looking around, I finally spot one. While Susan heads on, muttering about Egyptian cotton, I walk over to the assistant. When she turns around, I realise that it's Tamara. I ask her how long she's been here. She seems a little more awkward than usual, but she says they gave her the job a couple of weeks ago. I tell her it's wonderful that we'll be working together. She doesn't say anything to this, and just looks confused. Typical Tamara. She's probably forgotten all about the interviews. Her head is so filled with her many children. I would ask her about them, if I didn't think she'd tell me. She looks smart in her uniform, although she must be keeping the cleaners busy up here with all her scurf. I am about to warn Tamara about the child, but when I look around, I see that its keeper is dragging it off to the stairs, so I just tell her I'll let her get on, and walk over to Susan. We'll have plenty of time to chat once they've got in touch with me about my job. They'll probably put me in charge of Tamara, because of my O-Levels, but our friendship will always be a separate thing.

By the time we get back to the ground floor and find Judith, the scanner is saying that we've put nearly seven thousand pounds worth of goods into it. This isn't my fault, so I don't say anything about it when Judith asks if we're happy. As we head for the car park, I look back at the store and can't help but get a little excited at the thought that I will probably be arriving for work the next time I come here. It's been nearly a month, so I'm bound to hear soon.

17

FESTIVE

On the phone before I came over, Brenda said her goddaughter had been spending the whole day 'playing with her wee in the living room'. I said nothing because firstly it's not my place, and secondly I wasn't in the least surprised. However, I walk in now to find her dancing about in front of the telly and waving some bits of plastic around. She says you can play all sorts of games with these things. I suggest 'fetch' and moments later she's out in the back garden trying to find them.

In the kitchen, Brenda shows me another drawing her goddaughter has done. I can tell the blue circle with the red circle balancing on top and lines coming out of it is Brenda, because she has explained once before. The small yellow circle with a red circle on top, and yellow scrawl over that, is Brenda's goddaughter. But this particular piece of challenging art has a third mess of colour, next to the other two. It's a big purple circle with a red circle on top, and a squarish mass of grey scribble haloing that. I ask Brenda about it and she tells me that it's supposed to be me. I am furious, but I don't say anything. Brenda seems to think it's wonderful. She says I must be proud that her goddaughter thinks so much of me. I suppose it's just possible that the drawing isn't intended as an insult. She might just be pathetic at art. After I've studied the piece as a whole for a while longer, I decide to magnanimously accept that as the explanation until another, more obvious, personal attack presents itself. The back door swings open and in stomps the little madam herself with her bits of plastic. She looks up at me and grins. She is so difficult to read.

After we have all had some sandwiches made from turkey leftovers, Brenda gives me a small colourfully-wrapped parcel to open. It contains a red velvet box, and within that is a very nice delicate necklace with a silver pixie pendant on it. She says it suits my mischievous side. I don't know what she thinks she means by that, but I like the necklace and wear it immediately. Then Brenda pulls a mischievous expression herself, and says that when she was at the jewellers, she just couldn't resist buying herself a present as well. She shows me the present she has bought herself. It's a watch. It's a Rotary, with a white leather strap and a mother of pearl dial. It looks more expensive than my necklace, which casts serious doubt on her whole story about what she went to the jewellers for in the first place. Brenda is saying that the watch is water-resistant. She seems overly impressed with this. I suggest that she might have paid extra for a spurious claim. It probably says 'flame retardant' on the box too. I insist that the watch should be tested. Brenda follows me up the stairs to the bathroom, burbling about it not being important, that I shouldn't worry myself about it, but I assure her that it's no bother. The next couple of minutes are a blur, but the watch proves not to be flush-resistant. As we stare into the empty toilet bowl, there's plenty of time to think about how I could have tested the watch in the sink instead, but in the heat of the moment things get missed. That's just science. It's certainly not my fault, but I can't help but think Brenda is going to hold me responsible for this. I would give her a sad kitten card to cover it, but I've already used one as her Christmas card by drawing a festive-looking hat on the kitten and writing XMAS on its face. Hopefully that card will serve as some kind of example to her goddaughter with regard to drawing things properly. To cheer Brenda up, I remind her that she has yet to open her present from me. As we trudge back downstairs, I also point out that she has a perfectly good clock on the oven in the kitchen if she needs to know the time. In fact, she could just ask me what the time is, as I have a perfectly nice watch. I don't want to draw attention to that though, as it may seem like I'm rubbing her nose in it. Also, she might ask me for my watch. That would be very selfish of her. I'd hate not to have a watch. That's awful, if that's what she's thinking.

I've left my presents in the car, as I thought Brenda's goddaughter wouldn't be able to resist opening them immediately if I'd brought them in before lunch. Children are very greedy, especially at this time of year. I go out and bring them in while Brenda brews some tea. I put the two parcels down on the coffee table, and Brenda's goddaughter immediately stops dancing around in front of the telly, puts down her plastic things and comes over. I tell her to try to guess which one of the parcels is for her. She giggles and says both of them. Typical avarice. As Brenda comes in and puts the tea tray down on the table, I point out to her goddaughter which present is hers. She grabs it and greedily rips the brown paper off on the floor. She starts thanking me effusively when she gets as far as the packaging, which she tears apart in seconds, and comes up clutching the Clubstaz Stella doll I have bought her. Now that I see her out of the packaging, I am regretting it. Stella is dressed like a little whore, in a tiny crop top and a skirt that's barely more than a belt. It's disgraceful. I had seen the Clubstaz dolls advertised on the telly. It said they had attitude. It seems to be a bad attitude. Stella was the only one they had at the supermarket, and the packaging assured me that she was suitable for ages three and up. Mind you, it also assured me that she was a choking hazard, and I can't see her strangling anybody with those tiny hands. In fact, it doesn't look like she moves on her own at all. She is a pointless little slut. Realising that I have said this out loud, I explain to Brenda that I am talking about the doll, while she mops up the tea that she has just spat out. Her goddaughter is in hysterics.

Once Brenda has cleaned herself up, I hand her parcel over for her to unwrap. Her goddaughter is playing happily with her prostitute doll. She says she can't wait for it to meet Rachel and Bruce. Rachel is one of the other Clubstaz dolls from the telly. I assume Bruce is their pimp. Brenda takes ages over unwrapping her present. She is the complete opposite of her goddaughter in this respect, patiently picking at each bit of tape and carefully unfolding the paper. Is she planning to keep the paper? If I see it wrapped around my present next year, I won't be best pleased. Finally her gift is revealed. It's a lovely novelty salt and pepper set, modelled after Dracula and Frankenstein's monster. The monster is the salt, and Dracula is the pepper. If I was making them, it would be the other way around, but I'm not sure why I think that. There is a hesitancy in Brenda's thanks, so I assure her that it's exactly the sort of thing she likes. She informs me that they are just like the ones she has out on the dining room table right now. I tell her that this is probably where I got the idea. She says I bought her those ones as well. And the ones from the year before that. This is starting to smack of ingratitude. I remind her that I have, and use, ones just like them at home. I do. I have another six boxed sets left. I only wanted to get the one pair originally, but it had been my first go at buying things from the internet and I had got the quantity wrong. Brenda closes the box and says 'never mind', and with that, this ugly witch hunt appears to be over.

Brenda's goddaughter's face has just lit up. She's remembered something exciting. She goes to the cupboard under the stairs shouting that she has 'something for you' behind her. At last, a present. I don't quite understand how she didn't remember this as soon as I gave her the plastic tart. She returns with her coat, beaming, and rummaging through the pockets. Finally she finds what she is looking for and deposits a tiny bundle of tissue paper tied with a ribbon on the coffee table in front of Brenda. One small present. One. And it's for Brenda. I don't say anything, of course. It's not for me to point out the injustice at work here.

Brenda makes lots of cooing noises as she carefully unwraps the small package. She produces a tiny porcelain figurine from the tissue paper and extravagantly thanks and hugs her goddaughter, saying how lovely it is. She hands the figurine to me for confirmation of how lovely it is. The next thing I know, I'm stood in Brenda's porch promising to help her find it once the snow eases off a bit.

***

It's later in the evening and I'm being festive. I've just thrown a snowball at Brenda's goddaughter. Brenda is refusing to pour me another one.

18

THEATRE

I'm at a pantomime. I'm joining in. It's behind them. Now one of the actors has slipped over in it. Brenda's goddaughter seems to think this is very funny, but they're not getting back up. A girl at my school had to wear a rigid corset for six months after falling off her pony once, I tell her. Now she's crying with laughter. What is wrong with young people today? All I can do is shrug my shoulders at Prince Charming, who is glaring in our direction. Brenda is just looking embarrassed about the whole business, and she has every reason to be. Firstly, she should be a better influence on her goddaughter, and secondly, she should have got me the right flavour of choc-ice when she was at the refreshment booth.

The curtain is brought down briefly, followed by an announcement that the performance will have to continue with only one ugly sister. I tell Brenda it's a shame Beryl wasn't able to make it tonight.

19

SLIMMING

I've come along to the slimming club at the church hall. I'm only here to keep Brenda company, though. I'm watching my weight, but purely in an observational capacity. Bernadette and Maureen are in attendance, taking full advantage of the ten percent off they get with their neighbourhood watch membership cards. If they think they are going to get some decent biscuits here when they finish weighing themselves, they are going to be sorely disappointed. There are some oat-based things here on the refreshment table, but they are all packaged up for sale. I know this, because I opened the cranberry and orange cookies and the caramel crunches as soon as I got here, and they made me pay for them. It's a complete scam. I've had two more cups of tea than I had planned to have, just to try to get some value out of my membership fee. These biscuits taste like they've just had their respective flavours described to them at the factory. It's a struggle to finish the packets as I sit waiting to be weighed, it really is. And I'm being put off a bit by the whooping of a girl called Sally, who has just been weighed. She is what you might describe as 'bubbly', and she is jumping around and shrieking because she has lost three pounds since the last meeting. I'm imagining that it has mostly come off the brain.

When I finally mount the scales, I explain to Barbara, who is in charge of the club, that I am retaining a lot of water at the moment. It's true, I've had five cups of tea. She nods in an understanding way. As it's my first weigh-in, there's none of the shaking of heads and crying that goes on with some of the others here. Barbara gives me a booklet. It's a bit like an 'I Spy' book of food, where you get points for how much you can eat, and a personalised target for you to try to reach. Barbara says I can have twenty points a day, plus thirty-five flexible points that I can spread throughout my week. This means I can eat just under twenty packets of the awful biscuits per week, if for some reason we become trapped in the hall. The thought of this makes me feel a little light-headed. Barbara must have read my expression, because she says sympathetically that this can all seem a little daunting for a 'newbie', but that it will all be second nature to me in a few weeks.

I stick around to offer Brenda support during her weigh-in. She goes into conniptions when Barbara tells her that she has gained just over a stone, so I take my foot off the back of the scales, but it's too late. Her new weight has been recorded. Poor Brenda. Now she will have to have her points adjusted. Barbara says she was doing so well, too. I promise to keep my eye on Brenda, and Barbara calls me a good friend, which I am. I resolve not to get Brenda an Easter egg this year.

As we return to our seats, I spot a familiar face, just before it disappears behind a copy of the slimming booklet. It's James, from the department store. I rush over and say hello. He is very engrossed in the points booklet, but eventually I get his attention. He seems less confident out of the office. Nervous, even. I suggest that he's very slim to be coming here. He says that he has an ideal weight, and that the group helps him to stick to it. I tell him that I'm a little surprised that I still haven't heard from him about my job, as it has now been several months, and Tamara already has hers. Especially given how many more O-levels I have than her. James is very apologetic. He explains that he and Celeste got so wrapped up in discussing whether or not to contact the authorities, they forgot all about contacting me. I tell him that

I quite understand, and that I'm available to start on Monday, with no hard feelings. I notice that he's sweating, probably from a workout. He tells me that it's best if Celeste contacts me to discuss the matter further, as she is his superior. I advise him that my contact details remain the same, and we leave it on a friendly note, with me telling him how lovely it is that we'll be able to see each other at every slimming meeting from now on. He really does sweat a lot, now that I take a proper look at him. Perhaps that's the real secret of how he stays so thin. Some people are just blessed with their metabolisms.

20

RECREATION

I'm in the park with Brenda and her goddaughter. Her kite is stuck in a tree. It's still in the packaging.

It's a beautiful sunny day, for the time of year. Brenda's goddaughter and I are sat on a bench looking out at a small island in the middle of the park's pond. There are fluffy little goslings to look at out there, and it is also where I have told Brenda her purse is. As we sit and watch, she is rowing out there in one of the little boats they have for hire here. We would have joined her, but the geese look a bit cross. Inside, I'm a little concerned for Brenda's safety, but outwardly I'm laughing and pointing, so her goddaughter doesn't get worried. Especially after how much I was going on about how geese like to break people's arms earlier on.

The island is mainly a knot of tree roots packed together with silt and guano, so Brenda can't really get out of the boat for a good look around. I wish I could be more helpful in guiding her, but I can only really tell her where I was aiming when I threw the purse. I don't see what more anybody could do in this sort of situation, apart from warning her when a goose is coming. After a while though, once she's leaned over and peered into quite a few nooks and crannies in the branches, and been pecked a bit, she gets quite flustered, so it's my duty as a friend to try to help even more. I wander over to the stone bridge that splits the pond in two, to see if I can see any better from that vantage point. When I get there, I find the purse lying on the concrete. This is a difficult moment for me. If I pick it up and say I've found it now, It just makes it look like I can't throw straight. On the other hand, Brenda will probably spot me if I try to throw it a second time to get it to where I said it was in the first place. While I'm stood there, sizing up the situation with my foot on the purse, Brenda's busy-body goddaughter saunters over and starts screeching that she's found it, she's found it. It speaks volumes about her character that she's trying to take the credit for this. Reluctantly, I lift my foot to stop her tugging away at the purse beneath. I admit that it does indeed look like the purse Brenda had, but that we should probably check the contents to make sure. I'm really only delaying the inevitable at this point. To start with, the goddaughter can only find some money, receipts and keys, but then the library card and the Blockbuster membership emerge, and Brenda is rowing back to shore. She has a tense and slow return journey, as there is now a honking goose in the boat with her, so she can't make any sudden movements. As she eventually approaches us, I look through our picnic bag for something to distract the goose. Brenda's goddaughter and I have already had our sandwiches while watching events on the pond unfold, but Brenda's own ones are still there, wrapped. Without a thought for my own safety, I throw them at the angry goose, hitting it full in the beak. While the goose is greedily eating Brenda's two rounds of tuna and cucumber, she is easily able to make it safely up the other two steps next to the mooring point. Not much gratitude is forthcoming from Brenda as we walk back to the bench, but in a way, having my friend back safely on dry land is thanks enough. Then her goddaughter ceremoniously hands her the purse, and Brenda is full of gushing praise for how clever she has been. Unbelievable. In a way, I'm glad Brenda is covered in goose guano now. She deserves it.

On the way back to the car, Brenda suggests that I should buy her goddaughter an ice cream for finding the purse. She knows that I found the purse, not her, but without a prick of conscience, she's jumping up and down agreeing with this, shouting the odds about what kind of ice cream it should be, and that it should have a flake in it. While I go through the humiliation of taking the little fraud's order at Mister Whippy's van, Brenda stands some distance away, as she is covered in goose guano. Once the little madam has her treat, I order one of my own, and insist that the man puts two flakes in it. Before I eat my cone, I arrange the flakes so that I can flick chocolate V signs at Brenda's goddaughter. She pretends to find it funny, but she knows deep down that I've won this round. She must know.

When we walk back over to Brenda, it's clear that she's now unhappy about being the only one without an ice cream. Firstly, she didn't ask for one, and secondly, she's covered in guano. On the way back in the car, I look up all the diseases you can get from goose guano on my phone, and tell her all about them while I finish my cone. Histoplasmosis, that's one. You can get some nasty things from Cryptococcus laurentii, so that's another. And so on. She just turns up the car radio. It's a wonder she's lived this long, having such scant regard for medical knowledge. She's lucky I'm here to warn her about these things, and that's the truth. I just hope her current frostiness isn't a symptom of some kind of brain parasite from the goose doings.

***

Back at Brenda's. She relaxes a bit once she's had a shower and made a snack for herself. I don't even say anything about how long I've had to wait for a cup of tea. It's still sunny, and Brenda's goddaughter is in the back garden, enjoying making castles in the outdoor cat toilet she calls a sandpit.

21

EASTER

B renda's goddaughter is enjoying her Easter egg hunt. She saw me kick it, so she has a rough idea which garden it's in. Myself and Brenda are relaxing on her decking with a nice cup of green tea, which is very good for slimming. The club booklet says that it boosts the metabolism. It must be awful at this time of year for Brenda, watching everyone else eating their chocolate, while she's trying to lose all that weight that's on her slimming club records. It's certainly making me feel bad, sitting here eating the big chocolate rabbit she gave me. She keeps stealing glances at it and saying how lovely it looks. She drops heavy hints about how the points system allows her to have occasional treats, but I have to remind myself that this is just the crafty double-talk of the addict and eat faster. She says that I shouldn't eat the whole bunny, as that would be my whole points allowance for the day. It's my bunny, though. She can't tell me what to do with it. I'm already down to the front feet anyway. And in any case, I tell her, this isn't about me, it's about her own ballooning mass, which has been well-documented. She claims that she's a stone and a half lighter on her own bathroom scales than she was at the slimming club. I tell her that if she's going to believe faulty equipment, then she's only fooling herself. If I'm being stern with her, then it's only for her own good. I think I probably won't eat the two eggs I brought over in front of her now, though. It's just not worth the hassle.

Brenda could have been her ideal weight by now, if she had just taken Lent seriously, and given up dinner. I gave up the Sunday papers for the whole time, so that just proves it can be done. All it takes is willpower and finding something equally good to replace what you've given up. In my case, I simply bought more puzzle magazines. I may never go back. Sometimes that's just the way it is, like a couple of years ago when I gave up using VHS tapes. I found DVDs and a PVR were enough for me. That's how self-denial is sometimes, it just improves you.

Lent is over now, though, and I'm not sure Brenda has even forgiven me for Pancake Day yet. I offered to help her redecorate as well, but I think she was most annoyed about getting batter on her clothes. I've seen her wearing some of the things from that wardrobe since then though, so it must wash out of some fabrics. That said, the odour of batter does seem to linger. I don't think you notice that sort of thing so much when it's you though. She certainly remarks on it a lot less than other people do.

Later in the evening, we all sit down to watch Mel Gibson's Passion. Brenda doesn't think her goddaughter should be watching it, but it's the most quiet she's been all day. It's very moving to see the torment of one man on the screen like that. Brenda says he's not really Australian. Whatever he is, I can't understand a word any of them are saying, so it's a good job that there are subtitles. The devil appears for a bit, but it's not that scary. At least it isn't until Brenda's goddaughter throws up. Brenda is blaming all the chocolate and the excitement, but I'm not ruling out possession. She even admits that her head has been spinning.

I race out to the kitchen with Brenda while she's fetching some paper towels to clean up. I'm asking if she has any holy water, but she doesn't. My next idea is to tell her goddaughter that my gin is holy water, and throw that at her, to see how she reacts. Brenda just shouts this down as silliness. We'll see if she still thinks that when her goddaughter starts spider-walking down the stairs. I'll certainly be watching her like a hawk from now on.

***

After the possibly-possessed child has been safely put to bed for the night, Brenda pulls one of her proud faces, and tells me that she has something to show me. She pops into the dining room and comes back with some kind of misshapen clay pot, with flowers daubed on it. She says she threw it at her arts and crafts class. That's exactly what I would have done with it too. I tell her that it is very nice, though, because sometimes it's alright to tell a white lie. She says that Penelope, who runs the class, said it was the best one, and that Bernadette had agreed. My face drops involuntarily. I say that I hadn't known that Bernadette was in Brenda's arts and crafts class. Brenda confirms this to be the case, and offers the additional, unasked-for, information that Bernadette is 'a scream'. She goes on to tell an endless rambling story about how Bernadette's pot had collapsed on the wheel, and how quick as a flash she had decided that she was making a bowl instead. 'A bowl', Brenda repeats, laughing. This must be how Jesus felt when he was being betrayed in that film. Really furious.

22

WEDDING

It's my niece's special day. I've got a hat. I've been told to stop throwing rice until we get out of the car. It's not rice, though. That's not what they said it was in the bait shop.

The wedding is at my usual church. I make various gesticulations at the vicar to attract his attention, but he seems pre-occupied. Bit rude. The fiancé is up there with him, along with the best man. I don't know what they're called. It's never really come up. My niece is definitely called Susan. I've read it on lots of cards. Her handwriting is large and a little childish, but it is at least legible. She's still messing about outside the church. She is determined to make a big entrance, which is typical of her.

A hush descends, and then the 'Here Comes the Bride' music

starts up on the organ. My niece is making her way down the aisle. My sister's crying. I haven't done anything.

Susan is gliding down the aisle like everyone should be looking at her, like the big 'I am'. She looks like a toilet roll cosy in that dress. One of those posh ones though, like my Nan used to have, to be fair to her. My sister's husband David has scrubbed up well. He is walking arm in arm with my niece. I don't know if that's for support – is she drunk already?

The fiancé is smiling as they reach him. His face doesn't appear to drop when she lifts her veil. Of course, he's seen her before, so he's used to her. The service starts and my brother-in-law practically punches the air when the vicar asks who is giving my niece away. I'm trying to listen out for when the vicar says the fiancé's name in case I need to know it later.

Missed it. It might have been 'Tonker'. Is that a name?

It is a lovely ceremony, my sister assures me as we gather outside the church. There must be thirty pigeons pecking at my niece. They're going mad for those tiny eggs. The bouquet's gone into the traffic in the kerfuffle. That's about thirty feet. Nobody saw me do it. I don't know why I bother sometimes. The vicar is looking a little like a spare wheel now, so I throw the last of my fish bait at him.

***

We head on to my niece's reception in the bowling club. Crown Green, rather than Ten Pin. They seem determined to take up my whole day with this business. I tentatively try shouting 'Tonker' at the groom. He looks over, but in a way that suggests it isn't his name. That's going to bother me all evening now.

There is a big cake. There are two small plastic action figures on top of it. Someone could choke on those. Irresponsible. The department store has delivered all the gifts, and they are proudly displayed on the table furthest from the door. I'm imagining that is because they don't particularly trust their guests, and looking around, I don't blame them. A large number of the wrapped gifts are shaped like DVD cases. It seems like quite a lot of the guests elected to buy them the copies of The Exorcist I scanned in. There must be at least twenty, maybe thirty, wrapped-up copies of it on the table, and not that many bigger boxes. This isn't my fault. If Susan wasn't such a greedy so-and-so, there would have been more things on the list that ordinary people could afford. I hope she's happy with herself, I really do. What's-his-name isn't going to be able to make toast with The Exorcist. At least all this will make them appreciate the originality of my gift that little bit more. Having decided to ignore the list, I pop my gift on the table now. It's a Dracula and Frankenstein's monster salt and pepper set.

The couple take the floor for the first dance. There is something mesmerising about the spectacle of these two ungainly young people shuffling from foot to foot and slowly rotating on the spot. I make a mental note to take the figures from the cake so that I can replicate this scene later in my microwave oven. My sister comes over in an apparently consolatory mood and pats me on the back. She says that she is sure it will be my turn soon. I tell her I don't really want to dance with either of them. She narrows her eyes and smiles at me, rubbing my shoulder. I'm not really sure what's going on here, but it's making me a little uncomfortable. She finally wanders off, to my great relief, but not without a parting shot that she knows there is 'someone out there' for me. It sounds like a threat.

The bowling club is now filled with the elderly slow-dancing to 'True' by Spandau Ballet, and small children running around under the tables and competing in knee-sliding competitions, so I finish wrapping up my fair share of the finger buffet and pop outside for a breath of fresh air. The best man is busy spraying shaving foam all over what's-his-name's car. I join in and kick a wing mirror off.

23

SCOURGING

There are about forty people at the neighbourhood watch meeting this evening. This is unheard-of. The biscuits have been getting better since I became joint coordinator with Melissa, which accounts for a few of the newcomers. Bernadette and Maureen now tend to come along with a gang of about five others, all of whom come from Bernadette's sheltered accommodation complex. They aren't from the neighbourhood, but I've given up trying to stop them, as they have all paid up and swelled our coffers. That's not my view on the matter, but it's what Melissa and PC May say, so I've learned that power corrupts. Melissa isn't here tonight, as she is having some bowel removed. That means I have to give the opening chat and introduce PC Brian May myself. This is eating into my biscuit time. It's also the first time I've put the newsletter together by myself. I found out that you can photocopy your hand on the photocopier, so that's the front page. On the back, the top half of the page is just the usual advice about not leaving your front door open and bogus gas men, and for the rest I've typed up some of the crime that people whined about at the last meeting. I think it's all very professional, but I like the hand best.

Brenda and Beryl are sat near the front. Beryl has been threatening another visit for a while. Brenda doesn't live in the neighbourhood, but she said that she might come along for moral support. She's already had a cup of tea and two biscuits that she hasn't paid for, so that's hardly moral. I haven't mentioned her criminal record to PC May. As for Beryl, she lives about eighty miles away, so that's just ridiculous. She can't watch my house from there.

From my seat at the front table, I can see Mandeep from the other watch group arriving and shaking out his brolly. He waves when he spots me. He said he'd try to come to one of our meetings, which is all very nice, but that's another outsider coming in, eating our biscuits. Him and her from next door are attending their third meeting tonight. I could have filled the whole newsletter just with their grizzling. I had to edit them

124

down a lot, not least because half the newsletter was already taken up with the photocopy of my hand. Also, though, once I had seen everything in a list like that, it looked like a crime wave, and you don't want to talk up that sort of thing too much when it's happening next door. It can affect property prices.

I've just noticed that my niece and her husband are here. They recently made it clear that I'm not allowed to throw rice at them any more, so I've had to eat it all myself. It's helped me to keep to my slimming group targets, though. They don't live around here, but perhaps they're thinking of moving somewhere they can actually afford. What's-his-name looks like he has already lost half his hair trying to keep Susan in the manner to which she is accustomed. She is something else, she really is. Perhaps they'll buy some membership cards tonight. I could find out what his name is then.

It doesn't look like anyone else is coming, and there are no spare chairs anyway, so I stand up and clear my throat. I quickly scan the room to make sure I have everyone's attention. It's only after I'm happy that they are all looking that I realise I have been showing them all the finger while I was looking from face to face. I hope PC May hasn't noticed this. I turn to check. It's a mistake on my part, because now he's had the finger too. There's no way he's missed that. I take a deep breath, lower my hands to the table and open with a 'good evening' as if nothing has happened.

I'm midway through my list of things that people have found nothing better to do than complain about, when Bernadette leans forward and whispers something to Brenda, and Brenda laughs. Brenda almost never laughs, in my experience. She normally just acknowledges a joke by cleaning up after it. This is awful. I can't just let it go. I tell Bernadette that if she has something funny to say, perhaps she would like to share it with the whole room. In school, this used to work really well for Miss Parker, and Martha and Shirley would always shut up. Bernadette takes up the challenge, though, and she stands up and says quite loudly that I should stop doing readings from my diary and get on with it. Now she's getting more laughs, from around the hall. The smirk on her face as she sits back down is sickening. I tell her that is very clever, but I'm doing that thing where I cross my eyes and drop my lower jaw, so that she knows I don't really mean it. She must know.

I remember the other thing Miss Parker used to say when she was trying to stop people talking, and I ask if anyone else has anything to say before we move on. A lot of hands go up. My opinion of Miss Parker is worsening by the second. However, I am a firm believer in pulling plasters off in one go, so I point at the first hand I see, and say 'yes, you in the bright yellow poncho', as if I am on *Question Time*. I know it's her from across the way, but I can't call her that in my official capacity. She says that the man who came to fix her TV aerial found her wind chimes wrapped around it. All I can do is shrug, and say that this is scarcely a matter for the neighbourhood watch. She's saying that she thinks I did it. She's making a fool of herself, and she should concentrate on getting some proper curtains, instead of hanging ethnic throws in her bay. I don't say that, of course, because it's not my place, and I don't want her to put a spell on me.

Her from next door is next to join the bandwagon. She whines on about missing laundry, vandalised property, and a whole list of other things that she can only link to me by geography and opportunity. I challenge her to come up with a motive, because I certainly can't think of one. This feels like a witch hunt. Then him from next door stands up next to his wife, and pipes up with some ludicrous accusation of me putting my foot through their cat flap this morning. I ask him how he could possibly think that might have been me, and he explains that the back door is almost entirely glass, so the whole family saw me stride up their garden path and do it while they were sat having breakfast. He says I even waved to them while I was extricating myself. All I can do is shake my head, although that does all ring a bell now that he mentions it.

It takes me several seconds to recognise the next person to stand up. It's James, from the department store. He hasn't been to a single slimming club meeting since that time I met him there, and it really shows. He must have put on four stone, easily. He's still sweating, so that's clearly not helping him shed the pounds as much as I had thought. He has a sorry tale to tell about nuisance phone calls, both at home and at the office. Initially, I think that this explains all the times I got an engaged tone when I was trying to call him, but the more he goes on, and the more he points, the more it seems like he's talking about me.

So it goes on. After a few more loud complaints about very little, there's a fit of coughing from the middle of the hall, emanating from an elderly lady, as she rises to her feet. It's Madame Bucowski, the ghost woman. I'm thinking that this is at last a friendly face, but once she has balanced herself, she just points at me and says 'demon'.

This is all becoming a bit of a nasty scene, and PC May says that we should probably take a break for a cup of tea. He offers me a weak smile, but there's embarrassment written all over his face, and so there should be. These allegations have all happened on his watch. I excuse myself to go to the little girls' room and head into the corridor, shutting the heavy door behind me to muffle the jeering. They are all ingrates. It's becoming clear that I am going to have to resign as joint coordinator, despite the fact that half of the people whining here don't even live in this neighbourhood. If they were being fair, they would realise that most of these problems are for other watches to deal with. It's all a lot of fuss over nothing, but there aren't enough sad kitten cards left to cover it. Especially once I have left one on top of the mouldy pannier and other bits I have just kicked off PC Brian May's bicycle.

I haven't had my share of the biscuits at all this evening, but I can't face going in there again. I hope they all enjoy my Hobnobs and chocolate fingers, I really do. I can hear footsteps coming down the hall toward the door at the far end of the corridor, and I realise that it's time to leave. While these questions over my integrity have angered me, I have to go in order to stop this controversy distracting the neighbourhood watch from the many challenges it faces. I still have the keys to the hall on me. In a way, these have been my chain of office. I decide to leave them where PC May will be able to find them, sticking out of his back tyre. Hopefully we will still be able to be friends and see each other occasionally on a professional basis when I become a local magistrate. I know that this night of long knives and betrayal will only make me stronger. That's a lesson I took away from that film by Mel Gibson. I leave my post with my head held high. Without looking back, I push down the long metal bar and make my way out through the door marked NO EXIT.